# LET'S RIDE

# LET'S RIDE

AN EQUITATION GUIDE
FOR RIDING INSTRUCTORS
AND BEGINNING STUDENTS

*By* **Sue Henderson Coen**

South Brunswick and New York: A. S. Barnes and Company
London: Thomas Yoseloff Ltd

© 1969 by A. S. Barnes and Co., Inc.

Library of Congress Catalogue Card Number: 68–27242

A. S. Barnes and Co., Inc.

Cranbury, New Jersey 08512

Thomas Yoseloff Ltd

108 New Bond Street

London W1Y OQX, England

SBN

498 06705 X

Printed in the United States of America

# Contents

# *Introduction*

This book is a combination of three texts written by Sue Coen to accompany equitation instruction at her Windy Hill Stable. The author felt a definite need for a very simple, very basic book that would accompany this instruction without confusing the students with too much detail. There are many excellent books available today for the more advanced rider, but the beginner finds himself lost in a maze of confusion as to what he should be actually trying to accomplish as a beginner and intermediate student. Too much detail gives the beginner the feeling that there is so much to learn that he could not possibly become a good horseman in less than a lifetime so might as well forget the whole thing.

This book is not intended to take the place of good instruction; it is intended as a supplement to be used along with instruction to reinforce what is being taught in the riding ring. There is no substitute for actual instruction and criticism from a competent instructor.

## WHY IS RIDING INSTRUCTION NECESSARY?

Riding instruction is very necessary if the would-be horseman is to derive the most satisfaction from this delightful sport. Not only will he learn to ride correctly, but more important, he will learn to ride safely. Because he develops an understanding of what he is doing, he will enjoy himself immensely whether working a horse in the ring or trotting down a wooded trail. He will learn to love horses and to be considerate of their needs. He will learn to care for the horse and his equipment. He will learn to derive the most from his horse with a minimum amount of effort on his part and with the least amount of discomfort to the horse. He will be better able to achieve his goal of becoming an understanding horseman and a competent rider.

## WHAT ARE THE BENEFITS OF HORSEBACK RIDING?

Horseback riding is one of the healthiest sports, providing one simultaneously with the benefits of fresh air, the exercise of many seldom used muscles, relaxation, pleasure, and the feeling of being akin to nature during the many hours spent in the saddle. The city dweller rediscovers nature and satisfies his pioneering spirit as he blazes new trails through lovely woods and ravines.

Besides developing patience, consideration, and self-discipline, horseback riding also develops a real interest in something other than one's self. Children especially seem to gain so much from being with horses, for in their eyes, a horse is a real friend, something they have always wanted, something they can talk to with the feeling that it will understand them. They develop a sense of responsibility for the well-being of the horse while it is in their care.

## WHAT SHALL I WEAR?

Jodhpurs should be worn at all times for the rider's comfort, but the novice who does not want to involve himself with unnecessary expense may wear jeans until he knows he will be doing enough riding to warrant the purchase of the more desirable jodhpurs. There are several styles of jodhpurs to choose from, depending upon the type of riding, or seat, that the student is learning. One's instructor will advise the student on this matter.

Riding boots are the most desirable footwear but saddle shoes or other hard soled oxfords are satisfactory. Never wear tennis shoes! They are dangerous. The rider's feet can easily slide through the stirrups irons because the soles of tennis shoes are so slippery and they do not have heels. The thin soles of tennis shoes do not give the rider's feet the necessary support and learning the correct position of feet and legs is made more difficult.

## HOW CAN I CHOOSE A COMPETENT INSTRUCTOR?

Usually there is very little selection in this field as most areas do not support more than one or two stables; however, choosing the right instructor is very important for several reasons.

A good outfit for the riding student: 1) hard hunt cap for rider's protection in case of an accident; 2) Kentucky jodhpurs; 3) jodhpur boots (low cut).

If the instructor is incompetent, the student will not only be wasting his money, he will be endangering his safety. He may develop bad habits that will be difficult to correct later. He may end up disliking the sport. He may develop the wrong attitude toward the horse.

When choosing an instructor, visit various schools and observe the classes. The horses should be quiet and willing, well fed and well groomed. The students should show enthusiasm for their lessons. The instructor should show enthusiasm for her students and what she is trying to teach them. She should be able to easily explain the skills and the reasons behind them. She should take her time with the students, not pushing them beyond their capacity. She should have her classes under control at all times. Safety should be the most important factor stressed. She should be willing to spend some time with the potential student explaining the type of "seat," or style of riding, that she prefers to teach. A few winners in the show ring should be to her credit also.

## HOW MANY LESSONS SHOULD I TAKE?

Ideally the student should ride twice a week, never less than once a week. This is because he has so many seldom used muscles to develop and train. If the student rides twice a week for one year, he should become a fairly competent pleasure rider. By the end of this time, he should also have in mind his goals as a horseman: pleasure rider, show horse rider, trainer, instructor, breeder, or a combination of these. He can then continue his training with these definite goals in mind.

# *LET'S RIDE*

# 1. Let's Meet the Horse

As one is striving toward the mastery of equitation, he must also be trying his best to understand the horse, his disposition, general characteristics, and mental outlook.

First, and most important for the beginner to remember, is that the horse is a very timid animal even though he may look large and ferocious. His first reaction when startled or frightened is to run; if he cannot run he will kick. These are his only defenses and one must never forget them.

When approaching a horse, whether from his front or rear, always speak quietly to him to call his attention to you and your actions. Horses often doze with their eyes half open and may be thrown into a panic if they are unexpectedly touched. A quiet voice will give the horse enough warning to prepare him for your approach.

Because of this timidity the rider must develop his horse's confidence. A lack of confidence is displayed in the nervous, frightened horse that is expecting the worst at any moment. To develop this confidence the rider must be sure of himself around the horse and when mounted; he must know what he is doing at all times. The student will spend many hours in the riding ring gaining confidence in his own ability so that he is able to communicate this feeling of confidence to his horse.

Although the horse is not considered the most intelligent animal, he does have an amazing memory and a very good ability to associate ideas. He is easily trained because of this memory and his associating reward with correct action and punishment with incorrect action. Equitation is simply knowing when to reward and when to punish. The punishment is the squeezing of the legs or the pulling of the reins when asking a horse for a desired movement. The reward is the release of leg pressure, the release of rein pressure. It is most important for the student to learn that the reward must immediately follow the punishment, i.e., the reins must be released the very instant the horse halts, if not a half second before.

Because of this memory and ability to associate ideas, the horse soon learns to tell the feel of a passenger and the feel of a rider and will respond accordingly. Beginners are always passengers but with instruction, practice, knowledge, and determination will become riders.

The horse is very willing by nature—some more than others. He will do anything the rider asks *if* he understands what the rider is asking and is physically capable of doing it. Thus the rider must be definite in his signals and not accuse the horse of being stubborn when the fault actually lies with the rider. A foreign-speaking person is difficult to understand at first and to the horse, the beginner is a very foreign-speaking person. If the horse does not respond correctly, analyze the situation to discover just what is causing this disobedience. Blame yourself before you blame the horse.

The horse is born with a gentle disposition. His association with man may give him good reason to feel the need of protecting himself with hoof and tooth. A horse must never be teased or abused. A mean horse is a hazard and definitely a pleasure to no one.

A horse should seldom be fed a treat from the hand. A sliced carrot or quartered apple is very welcome, but should be put in the feed box. A horse loves treats and will easily learn to tease for them. This teasing becomes nipping and the nipping in turn becomes biting.

A horse has definite likes and dislikes and the rider should respect them. This does not mean the rider should cater to them however. The horse may have a definite dislike for a certain stable mate. Don't provoke him by insisting that he walk right beside that horse. This only creates a nervous, unhappy horse. The rider can, however, spend some time trying to quietly convince his horse that the stable mate isn't so bad after all.

The horse has a highly developed nervous system and is physically quite sensitive to pain. A sloppy rider bouncing about on his back, a sharp jab on his sensitive mouth by the bit, a sharp poke of the rider's heels in his sides will cause a great deal of discomfort. The rider must learn to make his horse as comfortable as possible with the extra burden the horse is asked to carry.

The horse has an acute sense of hearing and loud noises may make

A horse loves treats and will easily learn to tease for them.

This horse's ears express alert interest.

him very nervous and temperamental—again his timidity. A soft, firm voice must always be used; a loud shriek may be disastrous.

The rider should keep an eye on his horse's ears. They will often tell the rider what is actually going on behind that innocent expression. Ears flat back signify anger. Ears strained forward signify listening to distant sounds. Wobbly ears signify listening forward and back simultaneously. One ear flat back usually signifies a trapped bug; the horse would definitely appreciate its removal!

Because of the location of the horse's eyes, he can see in all directions. He can see a rider on his back. Sudden movements such as a coat being thrown down may frighten the horse and cause him to shy.

Horses are very curious animals. They delight in nuzzling and sniffing friends and strangers. They want to become acquainted.

Horses like to sniff objects which arouse their curiosity.

Horses saying hello.

Horses feel through their noses, so let the horse sniff any object which seems to arouse his curiosity.

These are but a few of the horse's characteristics, but they are the main ones with which a beginner need be concerned. If the horse does something which is unfamiliar to you, the student, ask yourself just what did he do, ask why he did it, and ask how you could have controlled or prevented such an action. Do not just shrug it off and forget about it. The more you can learn to understand about the horse himself and what makes him tick, the better horseman you will become.

# 2. Equestrian Fundamentals

## PREPARING TO MOUNT

Before actually mounting the horse, the rider must follow several necessary steps to assure his safety and the horse's comfort. (It is assumed at this point that someone is holding the horse for the rider.)

1. Walk up to the front of the horse and speak quietly to him. Move to *his* left side and take the reins from the person holding him. Always work with the horse from *his* left. This is the way he has been trained.

2. Check the horse's girth to be sure it is tight. This is done by slipping your hand between the girth and the horse. If there is room to spare when you pull the girth toward you, it is too loose. Your hand should just fit snugly between the girth and the horse. Tighten the girth by putting the buckles up a hole or two on the billet straps. (See p. 24 Parts of the Saddle) Be sure you are still holding on to your reins. *Never* let go of them. When using two hands, the reins can be looped over the arm. (See Illustration p. 21)

3. Check the straps on the horse's bridle. Be sure none of them are twisted, especially the curb chain—the chain under the horse's chin. Be sure every strap is correctly buckled. (See p. 134 Bridling)

4. You will notice that the stirrup irons are high up on the stirrup leathers. This keeps them out of the way during saddling and eliminates the possibility of their frightening the horse by banging against his sides suddenly. Pull them down the leathers. The stirrups should be adjusted now so they will be approximately the correct length when you are mounted. They may have to be adjusted later. This preliminary adjustment is a safety precaution so that the rider,

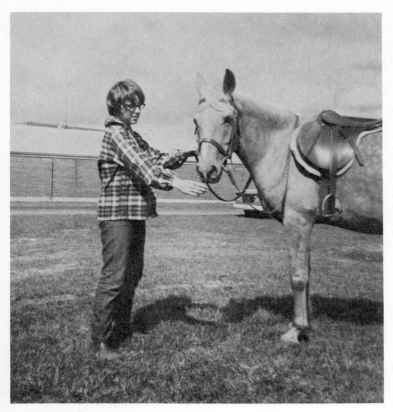

Moving around the front of the horse. Note the young lady's hands "walk" around the reins as she moves around the horse.

Check the horse's girth before mounting. This girth is too loose.

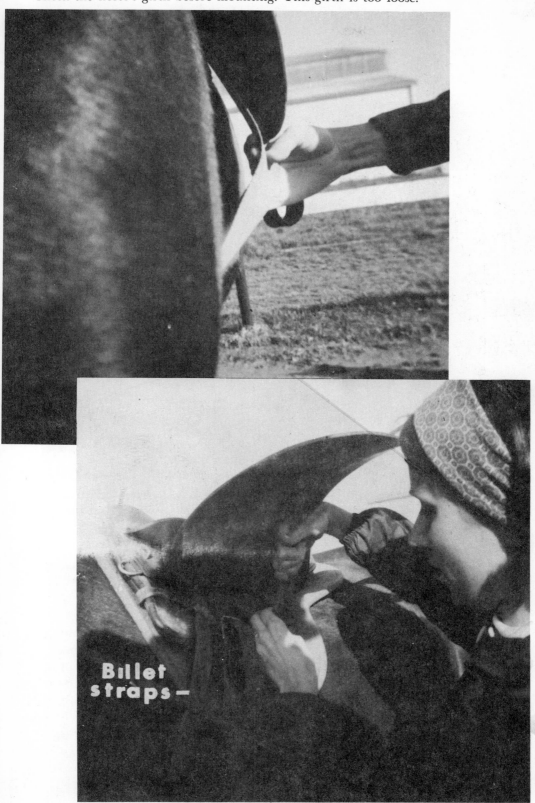

Billet straps—

When tightening the girth this rider has looped the reins over her arm in order to maintain control of the horse, yet still have full use of both hands.

Before mounting be sure to check the bridle straps. Note X marking a twisted cheek strap. This tightens one side of the bit and causes discomfort.

having just mounted, is not faced with some emergency and unable to put his feet in the stirrups because they are either too short or too long.

5. To adjust the stirrups before mounting, place your right finger tips at the top of the stirrup leather. Bring the stirrup iron along the underside of your right arm until the iron is against your armpit. It should fit, the stirrup leather being neither too long nor too short. If there is slack in the leather, shorten the stirrup. If the stirrup iron does not reach the armpit, lengthen the stirrup. Adjust the other stirrup leather to match.

Occasionally the left stirrup leather is longer than the right, and the stirrups will be uneven although they are buckled in holes of

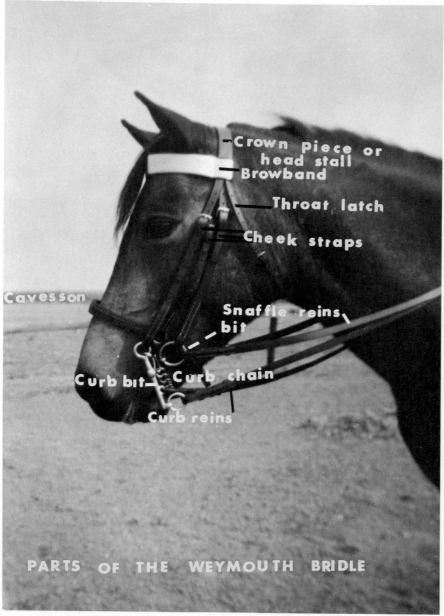

PARTS OF THE WEYMOUTH BRIDLE

The horse will be comfortable if all straps of the bridle are straight, the ends in keepers, and the links of the curb chain flat and smooth.

## PARTS OF THE SADDLE

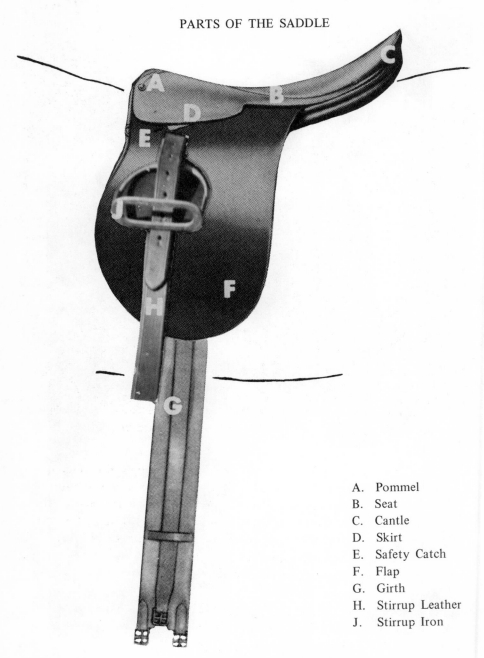

A. Pommel
B. Seat
C. Cantle
D. Skirt
E. Safety Catch
F. Flap
G. Girth
H. Stirrup Leather
J. Stirrup Iron

An English park saddle. Note the stirrups are in the correct position for saddling and leading the horse.

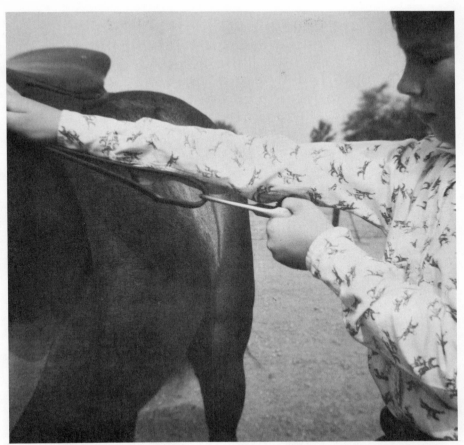

Stirrup leathers should always be measured before mounting. This leather is too short.

the same number. This is because the left stirrup is the only one used for mounting and eventually will stretch from the weight. A good idea is to occasionally alternate stirrup leathers; switch the left stirrup leather over to the right side of the saddle. This will alternate the strain and should result in even leathers. The stirrup leathers are easily removed and replaced because of the safety catch by which they are connected to the saddle. (See p. 24 Parts of the Saddle)

Throughout this whole procedure, the horse should be standing calmly and quietly. He should not be allowed to eat grass. It is impossible to tighten the girth or mount with the horse's head down. It is also very bad manners on the part of the horse. He will most assuredly take advantage of his chance to graze and will become increasingly more difficult to control.

This stirrup leather is adjusted correctly, as it reaches to the rider's armpit with no slack.

## MOUNTING

Although the rider should consistently mount correctly, as a beginner he should concentrate on just getting on the horse.

The horse should be trained to stand still for mounting, but if he insists upon moving, someone should hold him for the beginner's safety. Eventually, the rider will learn how to control the horse and mount at the same time.

1. Stand next to the horse's *left shoulder facing his rear. Some*

Position for mounting.

horses may kick out if they resent being ridden and you will be less of a target in this position. Also, if the horse should walk away while you are mounting, the momentum of this forward movement will actually help swing you into the saddle.

2. Pick up the reins at the buckle or seam with your right hand. Hold the reins up and away from the horse's neck.

3. Take the reins below your right hand with your left hand. Slide this hand down the reins to the horse's neck. The idea is to remove the slack from the reins so you will have some control of the horse while mounting.

4. Put the end of the reins (the bight) over the horse's neck to

Collecting or gathering the reins.

his right side, out of your way. Let go of the bight.

5. Your left hand is now holding the reins. With this same hand, still holding the reins, take a lock of the horse's mane in front of the saddle; or hold on to the horse's neck if the mane is roached. There are very few nerve endings at the root of the mane, so pulling it will not bother the horse.

6. With your right hand, turn the stirrup iron a quarter of a turn clockwise. Put your left foot in it. Be certain your foot is parallel to the horse's side; do not poke him in the side with your toe. Be certain to turn your stirrup iron correctly or the stirrup leather will be twisted and rub your leg when you are riding.

7. Reach for the cantle or seat of the saddle with your right hand. (See p. 24 Parts of the Saddle)

The rider's left hand holds the reins for control and a section of mane as an aid in mounting. The left hand should never be placed on the saddle when mounting as the saddle is easily pulled sideways by a beginner.

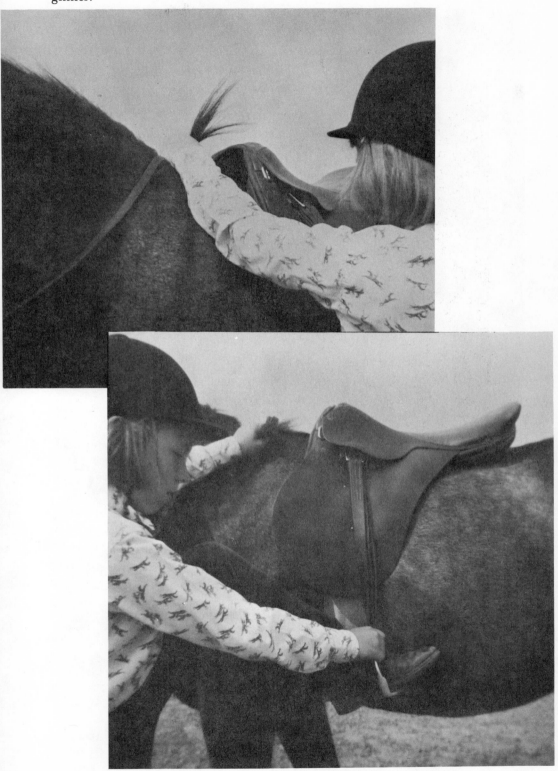

The rider stands at the horse's left shoulder facing the rear. She turns the stirrup iron a quarter of a turn clockwise with her right hand.

The rider's foot should be placed parallel to the horse's side so as not to poke the horse in the side with the toe.

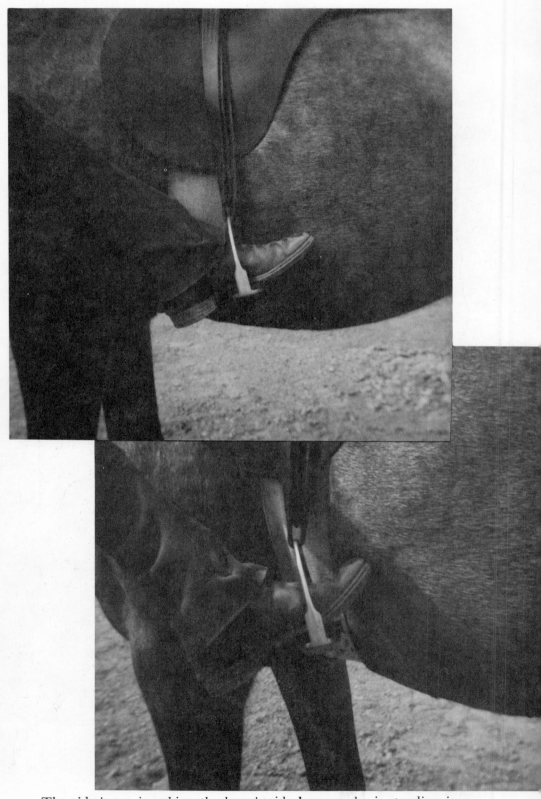

The rider's toe is poking the horse's side because she is standing in a position facing the horse's side instead of the rear.

This rider turned her stirrup iron counter-clockwise. When mounted the stirrup leather will be twisted as in the following illustration.

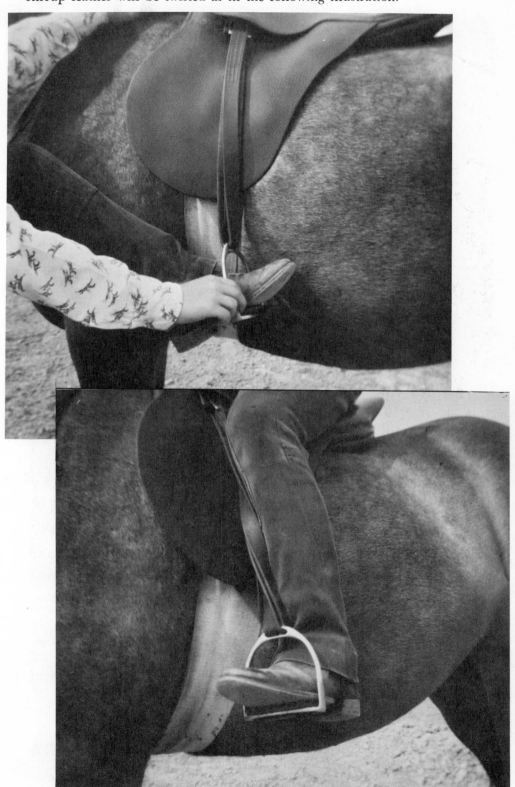

Stirrup leather is twisted because the rider turned the stirrup iron in the wrong direction when mounting.

The rider has brought her knee up over her foot so as to be better able to use the full length of this foot and leg when mounting. This skill is dependent on the size of the horse in comparison to the height of the rider.

8. Give several bounces with your right foot on the ground and spring up.

9. At the same time, pull with the hand on the saddle and the hand on the horse's neck and push with the foot in the stirrup iron.

10. When you have reached an upright position, standing in your left stirrup iron and balancing on your hands, pause a moment.

11. Now swing your right leg over the horse's rump. Be careful not to bump him with your foot.

12. Lower yourself *gently* into the saddle. Remember that the horse's back can be as easily hurt as yours.

13. Put your right foot in the stirrup iron and take up your reins.

The rider has placed the *front* of her knee against the saddle. When she tries to mount she will discover that she is actually pushing herself *away* from the saddle.

The rider is standing in the stirrups preparing to swing her leg over.

The rider swings her leg over the horse's rump. Note the maximum clearance of the leg. The rider in this illustration is actually out of balance and leaning too far forward.

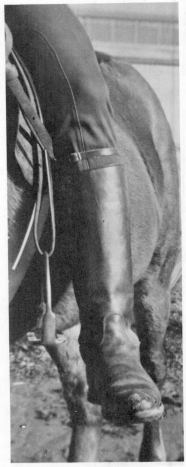

When measuring the correct adjustment of the stirrup leather from the saddle, the iron should reach to the ankle bone or a little below for normal riding.

This rider did not check his girth before mounting.

14. Check your stirrups to be sure they are correctly adjusted. This is done by taking your feet out of the irons. The irons should reach to your ankle bone or a little below for correct adjustment. Adjust the stirrups accordingly. (See p. 113 To Adjust the Stirrups from the Saddle)

15. *Be sure* that your left hand (with the reins) is on the horse's neck when mounting. Two hands on the saddle may cause it to slip down on the horse's side even if the girth is tight. This is especially true in the case of a fat, round horse and a rider who has to pull hard on the saddle to mount.

### HOLDING THE REINS—SINGLE REIN BRIDLE

One rein is held in each hand. The rein goes under the little finger and over the index finger with the thumb on top. Each rein is held firmly, without squeezing, between the index finger and thumb. The wrist and remaining fingers are relaxed so they can be used to tell the horse what to do through the reins. There should be a straight line from the rider's elbow down through the reins to the bit in the horse's mouth. This helps the hands and arms work with the bit. It makes the horse more comfortable because his head is not pulled into an unnatural position when the reins are used.

The rider's upper arms and elbows should hang from the shoulders in a natural position, close to the body but not tight against it. The rider does not want to look as if he were ready to flap his wings

A common error of the beginner—not holding the reins between the thumb and index finger.

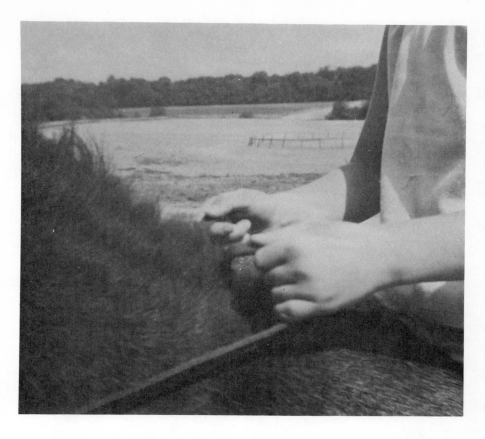

The correct way to hold the reins of a single rein bridle. Notice the relaxed wrists and fingers.

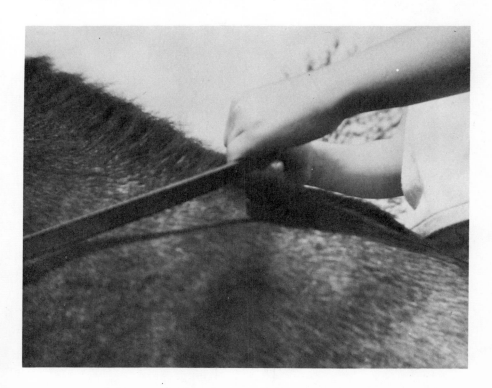

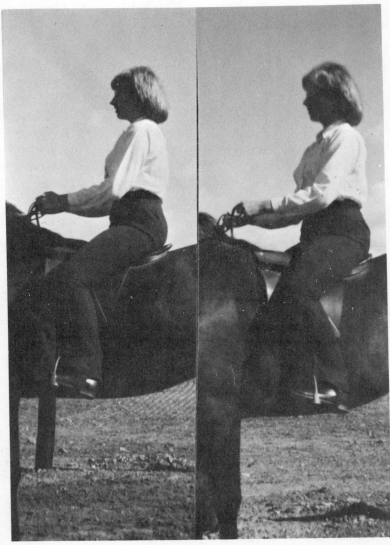

The rider's upper arms and shoulders should be in a natural, relaxed position.

and fly away. Neither does he want to appear cramped and tense. The rider must keep his hands, wrists, elbows and shoulders relaxed so that they will work as springs with the horse's head and neck. The rider will learn to "feel" the horse's mouth if he is relaxed. The horse will be more comfortable, and the rider will obtain better responses.

The hands are held about an inch in front of the saddle and several inches above. This will depend on the horse's head carriage. Again the rule of a straight line from the elbow to the bit applies.

The hands should be in a "thumbs-up" position, or with the thumbs turned slightly toward each other. They should be no further apart than the width of the horse's neck. They should remain im-

Reins held at correct height for horse's head carriage.

Reins held too high. The rider is too stiff in her attempt to sit up straight.

mobile regardless of what the rest of the rider's body is doing. The rider must develop enough balance to keep his hands free of involuntary movements which will annoy the horse.

The reins must never be tight, but they should not be allowed to droop. It will be difficult for the beginner to know just what length is suitable to his horse and because of his lack of balance it will probably be better if he rides with a loose rein in an enclosed riding ring. This will help him develop balance without using the horse's sensitive mouth as a balancer. It will also eliminate painful jerks on the horse's mouth. As the rider's balance and skill improve, he will be riding horses that require more control. The correct rein

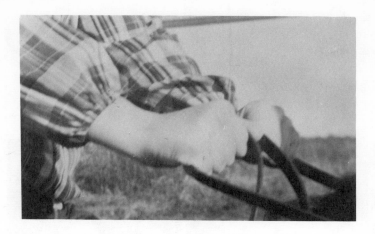

With stiff, unyielding wrists and fingers, the rider has no "feel" of the horse's mouth.

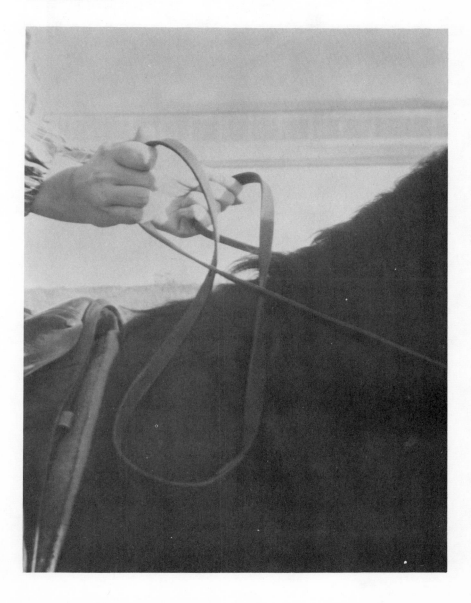

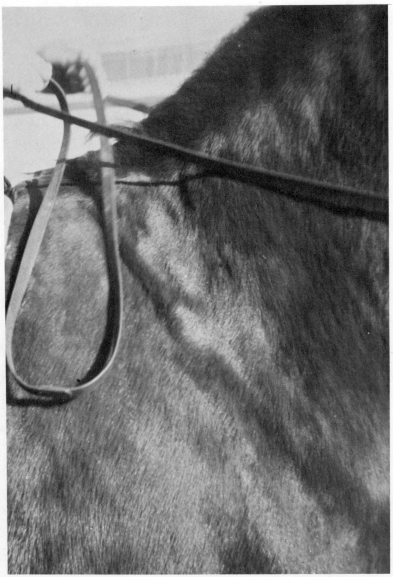

The bight (end) of the reins should fall over the horse's right shoulder out of the way of the rider when he mounts and dismounts.

length will thus more or less develop naturally. One's instructor, who knows her horses well, is the best advisor on this subject, as is the horse. If the horse tosses his head and frets, chances are his rider is creating some discomfort through the reins. If the horse is continually moving too fast, the reins may be too loose. (See "Weymouth bridle" in Glossary for correct method of holding two pairs of reins.)

## THE SEAT

The "seat" of a rider means the way he rides, the way he sits in the saddle. There are different "seats" which a rider may learn, depending on his purpose. The way a horse is trained will influence the type of seat his rider uses.

The "saddle seat" is seen on the high-stepping American Saddlebred show horses. The rider carries his hands higher than normal in order to keep his horse's head in an elevated position. He sits further back in the saddle so the horse can raise his front legs higher. A special saddle known as a "cutback" is used. This saddle is extra

Forward seat saddle.

flat and extra long with four inches cut out of the pommel to compensate for the very round, fat back of the Saddlebred. This seat serves its purpose in the show ring but is not practical for pleasure riding.

The "forward seat" is seen on the hunters and jumpers. The rider moves his body (and balance) further and further forward as the horse increases his speed (and thus moves his balance more forward).

Cutback saddle.

A special saddle known as a forward seat, or jumping, saddle is used. This has a higher pommel and cantle, thus providing a deeper, more secure seat than other types of English saddles. The saddle has "knee rolls"—padding at the point of the rider's knee—to provide more security over jumps. This seat is very functional for the purpose for which it was designed; however, it too is almost too exaggerated for general use.

The "stock seat" is seen on the western horses. A western stock saddle is always used. This is a functional working seat and serves its purpose of aiding the rider in roping and cutting cattle. This seat is comfortable for pleasure riding if the rider prefers a stock saddle; however, the beginner will be at a disadvantage if he learns to ride in a western saddle before he learns to ride in an English saddle. The bulk of a stock saddle provides little feel of the horse to the rider and he develops a false sense of security because of so much saddle. He is unable to use his legs effectively and efficiently because

A Western (stock) seat.

of the stiff stirrup leathers and the almost immobile stirrups.

The seat described in this book is called the "balanced seat," though this term is misleading. All seats depend on the rider's balance. Nevertheless the advocates of the balanced seat use this term for lack of a better one.

The balanced seat is a basic seat which provides the greatest ease to the horse with the least amount of effort on the part of the rider. This seat may be adapted to any type of riding.

Just as the name implies, the rider learns to balance himself on the horse by using various muscles. The rider learns to place his weight, and thus his balance, when and where he wants regardless of what the rest of his body is doing. Each part of the rider's body should be able to work independently or together.

A good position. The rider is sitting squarely in the center of the horse and saddle.

The balanced seat.

The basic position of the rider in this illustration is good; however, note the overly tight reins which cause the horse to over bend or over flex at the poll in an attempt to relieve the pain.

## POSITION IN THE SADDLE

In order to be an effective rider, and a comfort to the horse at the same time, the student must learn to maintain a certain prescribed position in the saddle. The points of this position are listed along with the reasons so that you may recheck yourself each time you are mounted.

1. The rider sits squarely to the front of the saddle. Any off center position would unbalance both horse and rider.

To measure correct seat placement in the saddle the rider should place four fingers between the end of the cantle and herself.

2. The rider sits in the deepest part of the saddle. Usually there is a four finger measurement from the end of the cantle to the seat of the rider.

3. The rider's leg muscles must be relaxed so that the flat part of the inside thigh, the inside of the knee, and the upper calf are close to the saddle. These muscles will provide an excellent grip when necessary so must never lose contact with the saddle.

4. The feet should be in a natural position, pointing almost

directly forward as when walking. This is achieved by keeping the inside of the thigh close to the saddle and the knee cap pointing straight ahead. If the toes point out and the heels turn in, the rider will be tempted to use his calf muscles instead of his thighs and knees, and thus his thighs and knees will be turned *away* from the saddle. This not only creates a weak seat, but will cause the rider to squeeze the horse's sides with the lower calf and heel to maintain

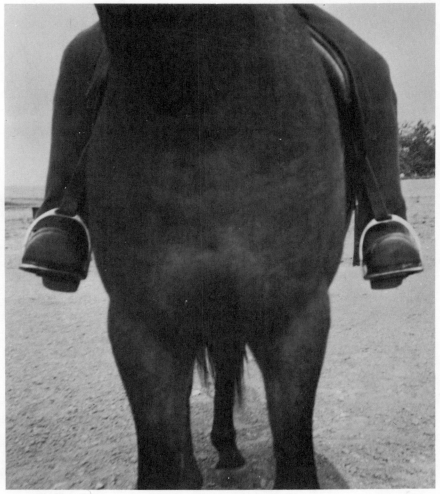

Examples of good leg position. The thigh and knee are close to the saddle, the heel is lower than the toe, the foot is in a natural position almost parallel to the horse's sides.

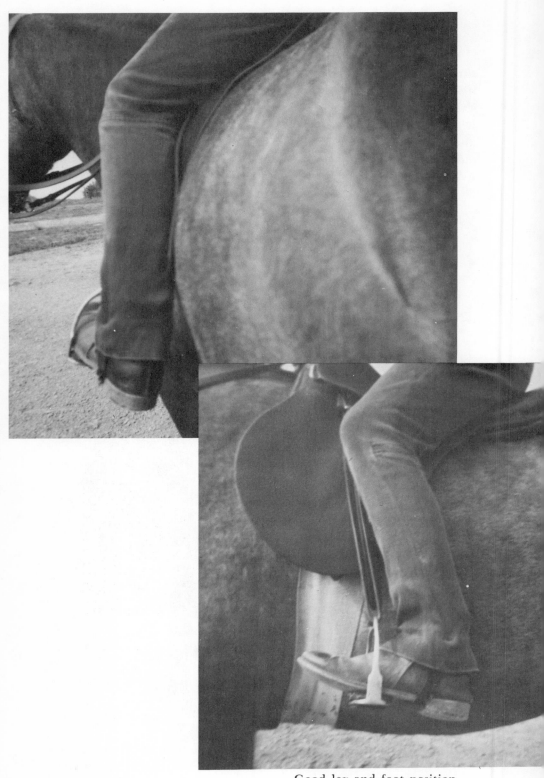

Good leg and foot position.

With the toes turned in too much and the lower leg pushed too far away from the horse's sides it is difficult to use the legs.

his balance. This in turn may encourage an ambitious horse on to greater speeds.

On the other hand, if the toes are *forced* to point straight ahead, as is occasionally advocated, the ankles may become stiff and unyielding and the lower legs will be too far away from the horse's sides to be used effectively and quickly when necessary.

5. The ball of the foot (the part behind the toe) balances on the stirrup iron. This is the strongest part of the foot and thus is the

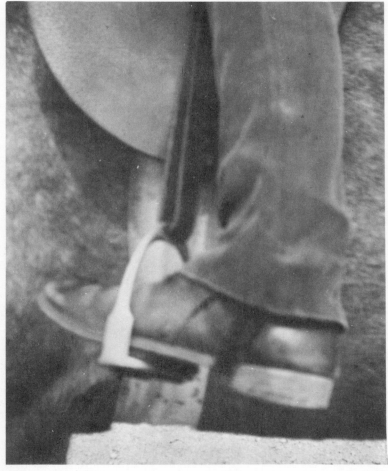

The rider has her toes turned in too much in her attempt to keep them pointing straight ahead. This weakens leg position and stiffens ankles.

part most able to support the rider's weight when necessary. The arch of the foot is much too weak to bear weight; the toes would be forced down and the heels up. If the toes are in the stirrup irons, they will too easily slip out. Remember that the ball of the foot is to *balance* on the stirrup iron; weight is not pushed down directly on the stirrup iron except when the rider is posting. This would prevent the rider's heels from being kept down and would cramp the ankle joints and feet.

    6. The heels are pushed down. This will stretch the calf and

thigh muscles down and thus make them most effective. Pushing the heels down will act as a brace for the rider. This brace will provide maximum support under any condition. However, remember that the heels are pushed *down*, not down and forward.

7. The feet and legs should be in such a position that the stirrup leathers hang perpendicular to the ground. The stirrup iron is the

The rider's foot is too far in the stirrup.

Pushing too hard on the heels stiffens leg and ankle and will push leg too far forward.

rider's "floor," and just try standing on the floor with your feet way in front or way behind you! When you stand, your feet must be directly under your body in order to support your weight and maintain your balance. This also applies to riding the horse and using the stirrup irons. Your feet must be directly under your body for the maximum amount of support and effectiveness.

8. The rider's back is straight but not stiff. The shoulders are down and back and the chest is out. This position promotes an alert

appearance of the rider and seems to give the horse the feeling that this rider is no slacker.

9. The rider's head is held up with his eyes looking straight ahead or in the direction he and the horse are going. A good bit of the rider's weight and balance are in his head. A lowered head not only pulls the rider's entire body and weight forward, but prevents him from seeing where he is going. In order to achieve precise control, such as during equitation figures, the rider must be able to see where he is going so that he may guide his horse.

10. The rider's hands are held as previously described.

## DISMOUNTING

1. Put the reins in your left hand. Put this hand on the pommel of the saddle or on the horse's neck. Put your right hand on the pommel.

2. Stand in the stirrups.

Standing in the stirrups in preparation for dismounting. Note that the rider does not crouch or stand with bent legs.

3. Swing your right leg easily over the horse's rump. At the same time move your right hand back to the cantle of the saddle.

4. Pause a moment standing erect, balancing on your hands and looking over the horse's back.

5. Kick your left foot free of the stirrup iron. Push slightly away from the horse as you drop to the ground. Be sure your belt buckle does not scratch the saddle. This will happen if you slide down the saddle on your stomach.

6. Another method of dismounting is to drop your left stirrup and slide down the saddle on your right hip. This places you in a position facing the horse, preparing you to take the reins at the bit to hold the horse.

Swinging leg over horse's rump; right hand will come back to cantle of saddle for balance.

Rider has weight on hands in preparation for removing left foot from stirrup.

The landing. If rider slides down her right hip correctly she will be in a position facing forward.

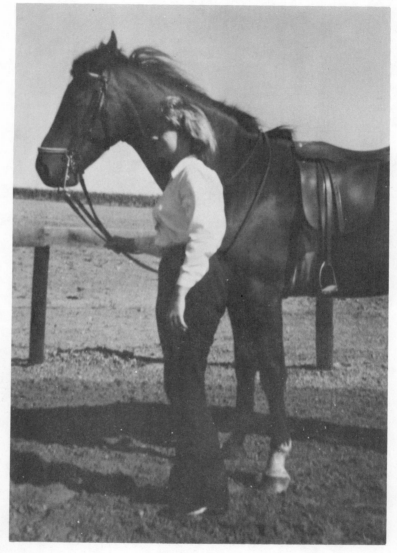

Having dismounted, the rider walks to the horse's head.

Unless you are very tall and your horse is very short, it is dangerous to step to the ground. This leave the rider in a vulnerable position with his left foot high in the air.

7. The rider should now slide his stirrup irons up the *back* strap of the stirrup leather. Tuck all loose straps into the stirrup irons. During these proceedings, the rider loops the reins through his arms.

Sliding the stirrup iron up the leather. Note reins looped over left arm for control.

Tucking the leather down into stirrup iron helps keep the stirrup iron from sliding back down as well as keeping the leathers from flapping around.

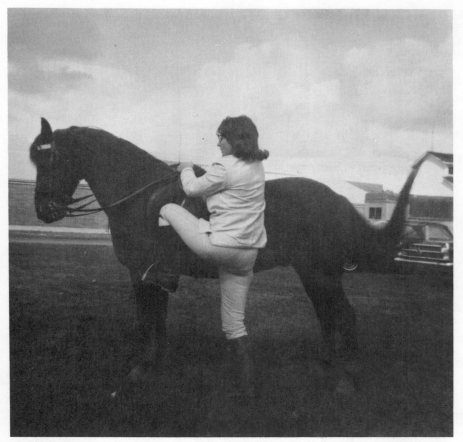

Dismounting by stepping down. Note the rider's vulnerable position at this point.

## LEADING THE HORSE

1. All leading is done on the left side of the horse. This is the way he has been trained.

2. A lead rope or lead shank is attached to the horse's halter so the one leading him will have greater control. For even more control, the chain of the shank may be slipped under the horse's chin or over his nose.

3. If a bridle is used for leading, the reins should be over the horse's neck. If he should run away there is less chance of them tangling in his feet and breaking.

4. The reins or lead shank is held in the right hand no further

than six inches from the bit or halter. The closer one's hand is to the horse's head, the greater will be the control.

5. The end of the shank is held in the left hand, preferably coiled. This keeps it out of the way and untangled so that it can be played out if necessary.

6. Stand slightly behind the horse's head, beside his neck. Face in the direction of travel. Do not look back at the horse or he may stop. Walk and the horse will walk. Halt and the horse will halt. If he does not, a gentle pull on the reins or shank will stop him.

7. Walk around the horse when turning to the right. Let the horse walk around you when turning to the left.

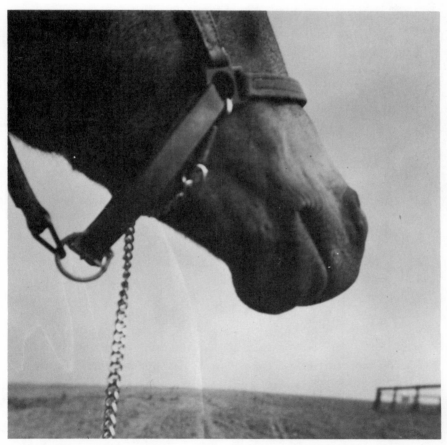

A chain lead shank under the horse's chin provides for greater control.

The lead shank correctly over the horse's nose for maximum control of a horse difficult to lead.

The correct way to lead a horse.

The incorrect way to lead a horse.

8. Keep in step with the horse. Keep your feet out of his way. He will not deliberately step on them, but accidents do happen.

If the horse is difficult to control, a short, quick jerk on the shank or reins is much more effective than a steady pull. The command "whoa" used firmly will also help settle the horse down. The horse should not be allowed to play when he is being led, but one that has been cooped up for several days can hardly resist the temptation.

# 3. The Walk

"Gait" refers to the horse's way of going. The walk is the slowest of the horse's gaits. The speed of a walk is approximately four miles an hour. The walk is a natural gait; every horse is born knowing how to walk. When listening to a horse walk, you will hear four beats as each hoof is picked up and put down separately. When a horse walks, his head nods up and down for balance just as a person will swing his arms for balance when he walks. The walk is the easiest of the gaits to ride because there is very little vertical motion.

The walk.

## TO MAKE A STANDING HORSE WALK

1. Collect or gather your reins. Both terms refer to picking up your reins and holding them in the correct position. They also refer to shortening the reins a little when preparing the horse for a new signal. This "collecting" will tell the horse "Attention!" and prepare him for a signal. If a horse is caught unaware, he will not respond promptly because he has not been forewarned and is not mentally organized for a signal.

2. Squeeze *both* legs against the horse's sides behind the girth. At the same time push the hips forward in the saddle. This tells the horse's hind legs to move; the hind legs *always* start a movement.

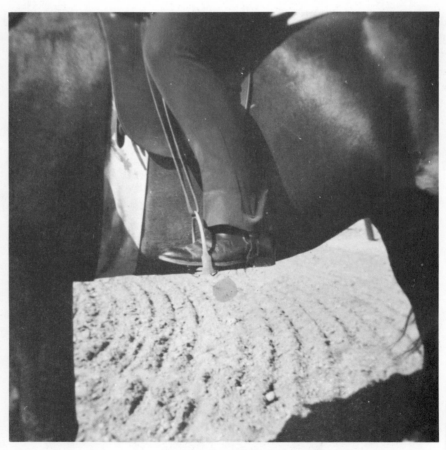

The rider is squeezing her *calf* behind the girth to encourage the horse to move forward.

The rider is using her *heels* (both at the same time) behind the girth correctly to urge the horse forward.

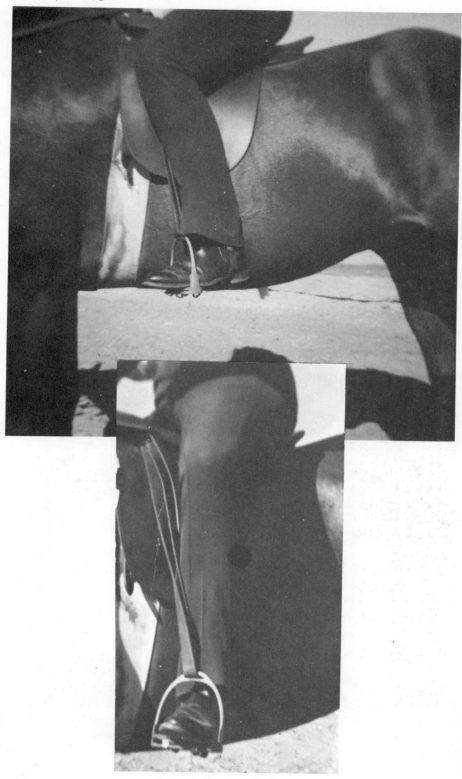

A beginner, when using heels or calves, often turns thigh and knee outward. This weakens the rider's seat as well as being less effective as an aid.

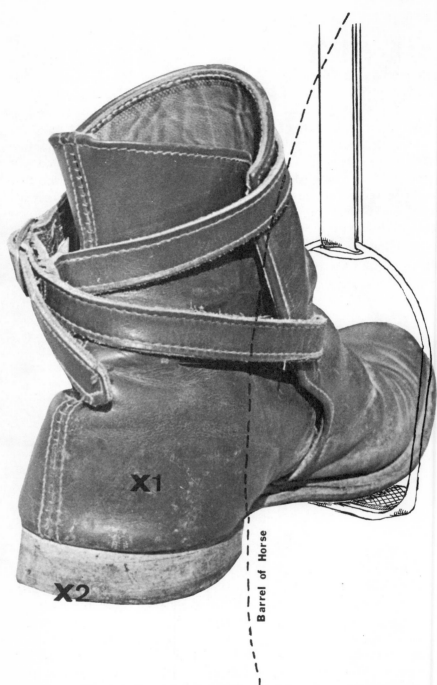

X 1 shows the approximate heel area normally used as an aid when the use of the calves is ineffective. X 2 shows the point of the heel which may be used even more effectively if necessary. A rider should wear spurs or carry a crop with an unresponsive horse as this is more effective and subtle than the unsightly heels constantly kicking.

3. The instant the horse begins a forward movement, relax the leg pressure. Let the hands move a little forward so that they do not jab the horse's mouth with the bit as he pushes his head forward. He must push his head and neck forward with his first step in order to get going. A sharp jab in the mouth is discouraging.

As soon as the rider is organized from the forward thrust as the horse begins to walk, he must concentrate on assuming the correct position in the saddle. If he relaxes his back, he will discover that his body rocks back and forth as the horse walks. If he relaxes his arms, wrists, and fingers he will discover that they move back and forth as the horse's head nods up and down. If the rider is tense, he will not be able to "feel" the horse's movements and thus will lack the necessary communication that makes for good control. The rider must be "tuned in" to the horse's movements so that he may interpret them and thus influence them.

## THE HALT

There are several methods that may be used when halting a horse. The beginner will do well to use an "active hand," the method easiest on the horse. Eventually he may learn other methods which require a more controlled rider because they could be quite painful to the horse if used incorrectly.

1. The rider raises his hands slightly. At the same time he flexes his wrists and opens and closes his fingers, squeezing the reins as one would squeeze a sponge, using just as much pull on the reins as necessary to cause the horse to halt.

2. As the reins are tightened, the rider pushes his shoulders back and his weight down and forward in the saddle. This is the same back and hip pushing movement used when pumping a swing. The rider will aid and strengthen his back muscles by tightening and stretching his legs *down*, thereby lowering his knees and heels. The rider is attempting to cause his horse to take a longer step with his hind legs and thus take a longer step with his front legs. As a result of this lengthened stride, the horse will push his head and neck further forward. His mouth will come into contact with the bit because of the rider's tightened reins. In effect, the horse will halt himself.

3. The aids (rein pressure, weight, etc.) are discontinued the instant the horse *begins* to respond. If he continues to walk, the aids are reapplied until the horse does come to a complete halt.

Rider flexing wrists to bring the horse to a halt.

4. The horse should not turn to the side as he halts. This may mean the rider applied uneven rein tension. It may mean the horse wants to turn around and head for home. Whatever the reason, it should be corrected by use of the legs and reins.

5. If the rider has used his aids correctly, the horse should be standing with all four legs squarely beneath him. The rider should learn to feel through his seat just exactly where the horse's legs are.

6. Do not use a steady pull when halting. The horse is stronger than any rider and can pull harder. A steady pull only numbs the bars of the horse's mouth so that he can no longer feel the bit. An active hand with a "give and take" action keeps the horse's attention and continually reminds him of the command to halt.

7. When the rider pushes his weight down in the saddle, he must not actively lean his shoulders back and stick his legs out in front of him as is so frequently seen. His weight goes *directly down* as his hips push *forward*. The legs are stretched directly down also by pushing the heels *down,* not forward, with more firmness. These aids must not be obvious; the communication is between the rider and his horse.

A beginner's attempt to halt the horse.

## TURNING THE HORSE

The elementary leading rein method of turning the horse is taught to the beginner because of its simplicity. The rider's hands through the reins lead the horse's head in the direction of the turn. The horse's body will follow his head.

1. To turn to the left, pull the left rein to the side and slightly back.

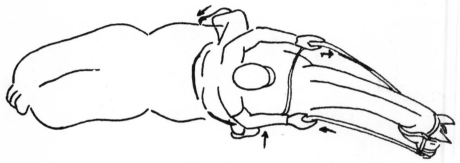

Direct rein—right turn. Note rider's use of legs.

2. At the same time, push the right hand and rein straight forward. This gives the horse freedom to turn his head and neck comfortably to the left.

3. The rider's hands maintain this position until the turn is complete. If the turning hand is unsteady, the horse will become confused as to just where his rider wants to go. The resulting path will be a pattern of zig zags instead of a smooth trail.

4. The hands return to their normal position when the turn is complete.

5. The rider must continually watch the path he intends to travel so that he is able to guide his horse accordingly. The rider must not forget that a horse is apt to wander aimlessly without a definite path beneath his feet or a definite command to follow.

Along with using the hands when turning the horse, the rider must also use his legs and weight as aids.

The rider's weight is shifted in the saddle toward the inside of the turn. He puts more weight on the inside stirrup iron and down into his inside heel. He puts more weight on his inside hip. The rider "banks" on the turn as when bicycle riding. The faster the horse travels, the more the rider's body must lean to the inside of the turn, and the more his weight must shift to the inside in order to be in balance with the horse's movement. The rider's *entire* body must shift position, not just his shoulders and head as is often the case with beginners. If the rider neglects banking on turns at the faster gaits, a loss of balance and a possible fall could be the result.

The rider must use his lower legs as aids when turning so that he will have control of and exert influence over the horse's hindquarters. The horse moves *away* from leg pressure. We discovered this when we were learning to make a horse walk. When the rider squeezed both legs against the sides of the horse, the horse moved directly forward to get away from this discomfort. During a turn it is important for the horse to bend his body in an arc with his hind feet following the path made by his front feet. The rider's legs and hands will cause the horse's body to form this arc. The legs are generally used as follows: 1) The lower leg to the inside of the turn is used at the girth to maintain a forward movement;

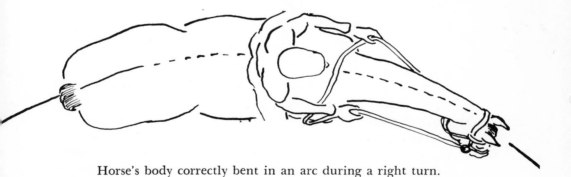

Horse's body correctly bent in an arc during a right turn.

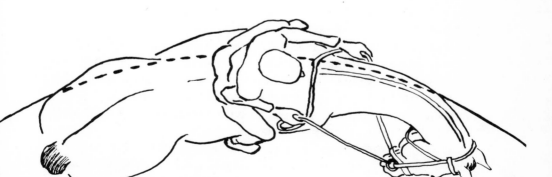

Horse's head turned too sharply to the right when turning.

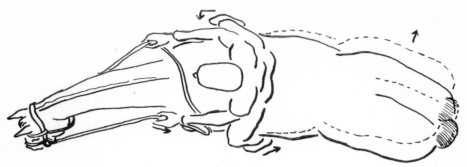

Turn on the forehand.

2) The lower leg to the outside of the turn is used behind the girth to keep the horse's hindquarters from skidding out and to cause the horse to bend around the rider's inside leg.

The aforementioned is generally used; however, if the horse seems to drag his hindquarters during a turn, the rider must use inside leg pressure *behind* the girth. This will serve to push the horse's hindquarters around the circle. The outside leg may remain passive.

It cannot be over-emphasized that the use of the legs is as important as the use of the hands as aids when controlling the horse. The rider should never ask the horse to turn by use of the hands alone. He is merely turning the forehand of the horse and letting the hindquarters shift for themselves. This results in a sloppy turn with the rear dragging along behind the horse in a less than desirable manner. Without the application of the rider's legs, the horse is easily able to avoid a turn if he is feeling disobedient. The rider must always coordinate the use of the leg aids with the use of the hands. The leg aids will create the bend of the horse's body which can be accomplished in no other way. They will maintain the impulsion of the horse on the turns. They will actually cause the horse to turn in many instances.

As mentioned earlier, the horse should be trained to move away from leg pressure. Moving into the legs is a form of resistance the rider should not permit. We teach the horse to respond to the leg aids by means of several exercises, one of which is the turn on the forehand. As the name implies, the horse moves his haunches around his forehand in a pivoting movement. This is easily accomplished by a beginner and will truly demonstrate to him how the horse will move away from his properly applied leg pressure.

The rider halts the horse parallel to the rail but about three feet away from it. The turn on the forehand is more easily accomplished at first with the rail to act as a stop. The rider begins to feel his outside rein only until he is able to see the outer corner of the horse's eye. He uses his outside leg behind the girth with intermittent pressure—pressure applied for each step the horse is to take. The inside leg is closed at the girth to discourage a backward step. The rider maintains a light feel of the horse's mouth to restrain forward movement, but not enough pressure to cause the horse to step back. The horse will begin to move his haunches toward the inside of the ring in a semi-circle around his forehand. The front feet move up and down but not forwards or backwards. When the horse is again parallel to the rail, but headed in the opposite direction, the movement is complete and the rider should ask the horse to move forward promptly. If the beginner has achieved even a proper step or two during his first few tries, he should be pleased. If the novice horse takes a proper step or two, he should be praised generously.

Usually the first few times the rider attempts this exercise, he does not use his legs properly. He attempts to turn the horse by strong hands. This results in an overbent neck and the front feet moving as much as the hind ones. The rein pressure must be very light, just enough to unbalance the horse and cause him to take a step to the side with his hindquarters. When the rider can accomplish these 180 degree turns along the rail, he should try a 360 degree turn away from the rail. Of course it is important that the horse is able to do a turn on the forehand in both directions.

The importance of proper use of legs is again demonstrated when the rider tries to keep the horse moving along the rail. As most beginners become aware, the horse will make all sorts of interesting attempts at taking short cuts through the ring as well as stopping in the center for a short snooze. The beginner also notices that if he uses rein aids alone in an attempt to hold the horse to the rail, chances are the horse's head will be aimed toward the rail but his body will be moving in an undesirable position diagonal to the rail. When working in the ring the horse should move parallel to the rail with his body bent slightly to the inside. The rider must be aware of this and use his aids accordingly.

Now to hold the uncooperative horse in the proper position along the rail, the rider puts pressure on *both* reins. This pressure comes back and toward the rail. The inside rein is an indirect supporting rein which will aid in keeping the horse's head and neck straight.

This inside rein must not cross over the neck. The outside rein holds the horse's forehand to the rail. The inside leg is used strongly behind the girth to push the horse over. The leg pressure should be intermittent or the horse may tune out. If the aids are correctly applied, it is most difficult for the horse to disobey them because he is held strongly in position by a rigid corridor of reins and legs. The legs and reins in this case could be considered as a wall through which the horse is not able to penetrate. Once the horse realizes what is required and that he cannot evade it, the rider has made a step in the right direction.

It might be mentioned here that it is very important for the beginning rider to learn to keep his horse on the rail. In the first place, it is self-discipline for the rider to train himself to be constantly aware of the horse's movements, intentions, etc. and of controlling his every step. It is also important to maintain the horse's respect. The beginner will notice that with each disobedience allowed, the horse will attempt more independent action. Soon the horse will be ignoring the rider completely. This insistence on working correctly along the rail will let the horse know that the rider is determined and must be obeyed. The beginner must not get the idea that the rail is there just to prevent the horse returning to the barn.

Moving the horse into the corners of the ring is very important. Here the rider may practice using his leg aids to obtain proper bend on turns. Do not let the horse turn when he wants to or from habit. The rider should always apply aids for the turn even though the horse has to turn anyway or run into the fence.

There are several other exercises favored by instructors to help teach a rider how to turn the horse correctly. These exercises will also demonstrate whether or not the rider can apply his aids correctly to guide and control his horse when executing a turn.

The first exercise is the circle. The rider is to make one complete circle. He must make the circle large enough for the horse to be able to comfortably walk around the path he is describing with no kinks in his back and neck. His body should be bent in an arc. The horse should maintain an even speed throughout this figure; no speeding up or slowing down. The rider must use his aids accordingly to achieve this.

When the rider can execute correct circles to the left and right, he is ready to learn the Figure 8. The Figure 8 is two *circles* joined together in the center. The rider begins this figure by proceeding to the center of the two circles he is to describe. He halts just long

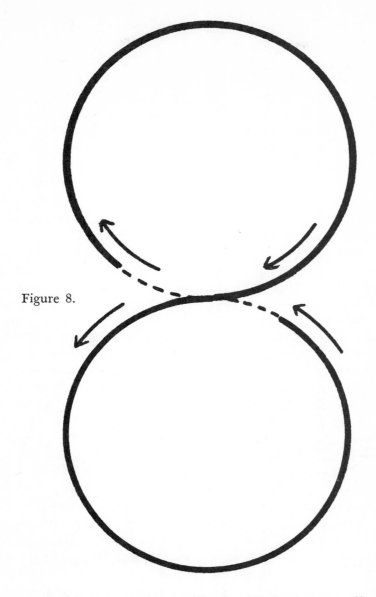

Figure 8.

enough to plan the path he will take. He begins to walk (trot or canter as the case may be) *straight* ahead. When the horse has taken a stride or two, the rider begins to bend him either to the left or right; this is the rider's decision unless otherwise instructed. The rider completes this circle as he returns to his starting point and describes a circle of the same shape and size in the other direction. When he has completed this second circle, he halts at the starting point. This is to indicate the figure is complete. Only one figure need be described unless otherwise instructed. The rider must very carefully plan the size and shape of his circles so that they are *circles* and not tear drops, and so that they are of the same size. As the rider's skill develops, he will begin to do these figures at the trot and later the canter. These are discussed in a later chapter.

When the rider can turn the horse correctly in good form with good control using the leading rein, he may begin to learn the more subtle direct rein method for turning the horse. This is a more severe, and thus could be a more painful, method if not executed properly because there is more *direct* pressure on the bars of the horse's mouth.

This rider is turning her horse to the right. Notice active right hand and passive left hand.

Shortening the left rein.

Instead of bringing the turning hand out to the side as in the leading rein, the rider closes his fingers, flexes his wrists and brings his turning hand straight back as little or as much as necessary until the horse begins to turn. The hand may be fixed in this position until the turn is complete, or the rider may continuously squeeze the turning rein by opening and closing his fingers in rhythm with the horse's stride. This intermittent pressure will remind the horse of what he has been asked to do, and in the case of a stiff, inflexible horse, will cause him to bend his head and neck when executing a turn.

The trot. Excellent position for walk and sitting trot. Note the good balance and collection of the horse. Notice how the rider is using the snaffle (top) reins by tightening or flexing her little fingers.

This pressure applied directly to the bars of the horse's mouth must be a very light, even pressure. Too much pressure will cause discomfort, rebellion, and a badly executed turn. The rider must strive to achieve rein work so subtle that it would take the most experienced eye to detect this communication to the horse. Of course the legs and weight will aid the hands during this procedure.

## FLEXING THE WRISTS

The rider flexes his wrists by turning his hands in such a position that the thumbs tilt forward as the little fingers are turned back toward the rider. This flexing is a smoother rein action than pulling the reins with the entire arms, an action which not only looks unsightly, but is wasted motion for the rider. Flexible wrists and fingers will provide the rider with a soft feel of the horse's mouth. The rider should strive to develop very sensitive fingers so he can achieve very delicate control. A well trained horse will respond to delicate control, whereas he may resent force. The trainer of a colt always works very patiently teaching his student to respond to lighter and lighter aids.

## TO SHORTEN OR LENGTHEN THE REINS

Occasionally as a beginner the rider will discover his reins are too long for proper control. He cannot use them without punching himself in the stomach. Perhaps the horse does not want to turn in the direction his rider plans to go and the rider requires more control, achieved only through a shortened turning rein. This is how the reins are shortened (left rein):

1. Pick up the left rein where it comes over the left index finger with the index finger and thumb of the right hand. Hold that rein in place with these fingers while you slide your left hand down the rein toward the horse's head to the desired length.

2. Take your finger and thumb off the rein. Shorten the right rein. Remember, do not release the rein you are *not* shortening.

The reins are lengthened by sliding the hands *back* on the reins to the desired length. Be careful not to pull the horse's mouth while doing this.

# 4. The Trot

The trot is another of the horse's natural gaits. Horses that trot are born knowing how to trot. The trot is a two-beat gait of three speeds—the slow or jog trot of about 6 m.p.h., the medium speed or ordinary trot of about 8 m.p.h., and the fast, extended trot of about 10 to 12 m.p.h. The very fast extended trot is demonstrated by the Standardbred horses that race in harness. A saddle horse does not trot this fast.

As the horse trots the rider can hear a definite two-beat rhythm. This is because one front foot and the *diagonally opposite* hind foot move forward, down, back, and up at the same time. The trot is thus described as a diagonal gait. The rider will bounce when the horse trots because the horse's backbone goes up and down with each stride. When the horse jogs, a very slow trot, the rider can learn to sit very comfortably. When the horse trots faster the rider may "post." This will be explained later.

## SIGNALS FOR THE TROT

1. Shorten the reins slightly and tighten the legs for "Attention!" The rider shortens his reins before trotting not only to prepare the horse for a signal, but because the horse will tuck his chin in further than when walking and the walking reins will be too long for good control.

2. The rider pushes his hands forward and squeezes his calves or bumps the horse behind the girth with both heels. If the horse does not trot immediately, the legs and heels are used harder. The hands

are pushed forward with the first stride because the horse will push his head and neck out with this step in order to gain speed; if he should run into the bit, he may return to a walk.

After this first stride, the rider returns his hands to their normal position. He will notice that the horse's head maintains a steady position when trotting. The rider's hands must also maintain a steady position and not follow the movements of his body.

A stiff legged, tense rider attempting to sit the trot.

## THE SITTING TROT

The rider is able to sit to the slow trot easier than to post to it; however, he must first develop the ability to relax his body and push his spine down into the saddle as when halting. The spine, knees and ankles are shock absorbers that will provide a comfortable ride for the rider who learns to keep these joints relaxed so that they *may* absorb the jolts. The rider may push a little on his heels so that he will not lose his stirrups, but his feet must balance in the stirrups without the weight pushing directly down onto them. This will only cause the rider's joints to stiffen. Stiff joints will push the rider out of the saddle.

It is very important for the rider to learn to sit the trot well before he goes on to other skills. If the rider neglects this important lesson, he will be unable to develop his maximum balance and will have difficulty learning to sit a canter. A great deal of training of the horse is done at a sitting trot, rather than posting, because the rider has a greater feel, and thus can provide a greater influence over the horse's movements. Thus it is undoubtedly one of the most important foundation skills for the beginner to learn.

## POSTING TO THE TROT

In order to provide greater comfort to both horse and rider by eliminating the almost unavoidable bouncing in the saddle, the rider may "post" as the horse executes an ordinary or fast (extended) trot. Posting is the rising and sitting, of the rider in rhythm with the 1-2-1-2 beat of the diagonal trot. The rider rises on 1, sits on 2, rises on 1, and so forth. The rider may watch one shoulder of the horse. As it moves forward, the rider rises by tightening his knees and putting more weight in his stirrups and heels; as it moves back, the rider sits gently down by rolling back on his thighs. The rider's knee becomes a pivot point—an imaginary axle goes through the horse, saddle, and rider's knees. As the rider rises, the angle behind his knee opens; as he returns to the saddle, it closes. The angle at the rider's elbow will also open and close as the rider's hands remain in a steady position. The rider must not let them follow his body movements as he posts.

The rider's position at a posting trot remains as it was during the walk and sitting trot with one exception—as the horse executes an extended (very fast) trot, his weight will move further forward

Posting correctly.

Posting incorrectly. The rider's legs are too far forward, making it difficult for her to rise out of the saddle.

for speed. The rider's weight must do the same so that he will remain in balance with the horse. This more forward position is accomplished by tilting the body forward *from the hips,* not by bending the shoulders and head further forward. The angle of the rider's entire torso is the only change made.

Some of the pitfalls a beginner should be aware of when learning to post are as follows:

1. The beginner may have difficulty catching the rhythm of the trot unless he has spent a good deal of time practicing the sitting trot. This fault may be remedied by spending more time sitting and counting the beats.

2. The rider must take care not to return to the saddle too soon after rising or he will sit just in time to feel the bounce he rose out of the saddle to avoid. This is usually a sign of incorrect or weak leg position, lack of rhythm, or lack of balance because the stirrups are too long.

3. The rider must be certain that his legs are directly under his body or he will have difficulty rising out of the saddle. If the rider's legs are too far forward they will swing back and forth, or pump, as the rider posts. This is to be avoided because it is tiring for the rider and annoying to the horse.

If the rider's legs are too far back, or his heels are up, he will tip forward as he rises. This loss of balance can be somewhat unnerving.

4. The rider must do his best not to rise too far out of the saddle. He is to leave the saddle just enough to avoid the bounce, no higher. A beginner is apt to try to stand straight up in the stirrups, thinking this is what is expected.

5. As the rider returns to the saddle, he must not thump down hard—think of the poor horse's back! The rider rolls gently back on his thighs, a movement comfortable to the horse as well as the rider. This takes greater leg control and thus more practice.

6. The rider must be sure he *does* return to the saddle; otherwise he will be unable to feel the forward thrust the horse's legs provide. This thrust gives the relaxed rider the necessary push out of the saddle, and he will not have to expend energy to actively rise out of the saddle. A stiff, tense rider often holds himself slightly out of the saddle just enough to be unfeeling of his helpful horse.

7. The rider must be sure to keep his shoulders back and his back straight; they must not be rounded as the rider rises.

8. The rider must not try to lift his body out of the saddle by pulling up his shoulders. His feet provide the lifting.

Rider attempting to post using the hands. Note the weak leg position.

9. The rider must keep his arms still; do not let them flap up and down with the body movements.

10. The rider does not balance with his hands, nor does he pull himself up by the reins. When he posts, the rider's hands must remain passive until the time he has become skilled enough to use them actively in influencing the horse.

11. The rider must keep his entire torso in alignment as he rises. Occasionally a beginner will try to rise from his hips alone. He then simply throws them forward as he rises. This is unsightly and tiresome.

12. The beginner may rise too high or too straight and thus be

Posting on the left (correct) or outside diagonal.

"left behind"; in other words, he returns to the saddle a fraction of a second too late and feels that he may fall backwards off the horse.

13. The rider should sit the first three or four beats of the trot before posting so that he knows the horse *is* trotting and not executing another gait.

14. As the rider returns to the saddle, his knees must remain close to the saddle. Do not let them pop away from the saddle. This weakens the rider's position.

The beginner will discover that a horse with a smooth trot is often more difficult to post to than a horse with a strong, rough trot. This is because a rough horse actually causes the rider to post by providing a very definite upward thrust which pushes the rider out of the saddle. A smooth trotting horse provides less of a thrust and the rider must more actively cause himself to post.

If the horse is lame or does not have a good "square" trot, the rider will also have difficulty posting. The rider posts only when the horse trots. There are several other gaits of the same speed as the trot that the beginner may interpret as a trot, but the rider does not post to these. If the rider must strain and struggle to post, he should realize that chances are the horse is *not* trotting.

### THE DIAGONALS

As the horse trots, his diagonal pairs of legs move together—the right front and left hind work as a pair as do the left front and right hind. The trot is a diagonal gait because of the diagonal line described by each pair of legs.

As the rider posts, he must rise as one diagonal pair of legs moves forward and sit as that *same* pair of diagonal legs moves back. The rider will watch his horse's shoulders—watching his legs would be most difficult. If the rider is rising as the horse's *right* shoulder (and leg) is moving forward, he is posting on the "right diagonal"; if he rises as the horse's *left* shoulder (and leg) moves forward, he is posting on the "left diagonal." In a riding ring, one always posts on the "outside diagonal"; that is, when the horse's shoulder (and leg) *next to the fence* moves forward, the rider rises. As it moves back, he sits down.

Now the question arises as to what one should do upon the discovery that he is posting on the incorrect, or inside, diagonal in the ring. To change his diagonal, the rider sits *one beat* of the trot. Instead of rising with the right diagonal as he has been doing, the rider merely sits until he feels one bump, then rises; he should be posting on the left diagonal. The rider must be certain he sits an uneven number of bounces; should he sit an even number, he will discover he is still posting on the diagonal he is attempting to change. He must be certain to sit a *complete* beat. Occasionally a tense rider will sit a half beat and thus remain posting on the same diagonal. The rider must be aware also of the fact that the horse can cause the rider to change his diagonal by stumbling, shying or some other act which may cause the rider to sit a few beats of the trot in order to regain his balance.

As the diagonals become more easily recognized, the rider should

Posting on the right (correct) or outside diagonal.

learn to spot the correct one with just a downward glance to the horse's shoulder. An obvious stare directed from one shoulder to the other not only signifies a beginner, it gives the horse too much freedom in his choice of direction. The rider must not forget that the horse needs constant control. An excellent rider has learned to feel on which diagonal he is posting.

There are several good reasons for posting on the outside diagonal in the riding ring as well as for changing diagonals at all:

1. Posting on the outside diagonal is required in equitation classes in the show ring. Equitation classes are classes where the rider is judged on his or her ability to ride correctly.

Diagram of the serpentine.

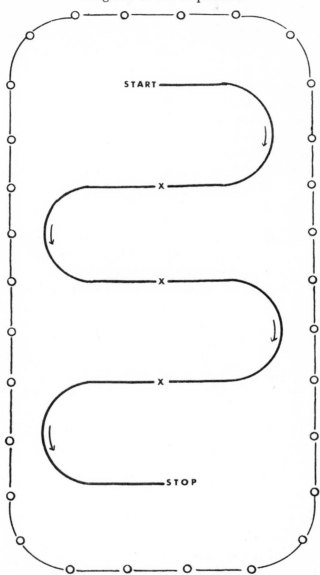

2. Posting on the outside diagonal keeps the rider's inside leg steadier on turns.

3. Posting on the outside diagonal keeps the horse's trot steadier on turns.

4. To change diagonals as the rider changes direction evenly develops the muscles on both sides of the horse. The horse whose rider

posts only on the right diagonal, for instance, will develop a strong left side, as this is the weight-bearing side. He may even refuse to canter on the right lead because of this.

5. On a trail ride, changing diagonals will rest both the horse and rider. The horse is able to rest because he will utilize a different set of muscles when bearing the rider's weight. This will provide a different feel to the rider, thus resting him. As the rider becomes aware of the two diagonals he will discover that one diagonal may be easier for him to post to on a particular horse. This may be because one side of the horse's body is stronger than the other and is thus able to bear weight easier. It may be because the rider has posted too much on one diagonal to the neglect of the other, and finds that it is difficult to post on the other without feeling a twisting motion in the hips.

As soon as the rider can readily detect on which diagonal he is posting, he is ready to begin learning to execute various equitation figures that will require a change of diagonals.

The circle should be practiced first. The rider does not change diagonals during this figure because he does not change directions; however, this figure will help him develop balance on turns while posting. If the horse should attempt to slow down during figure work, the rider can maintain the trot by using his legs *as he sits* during the posting sequence.

The Figure 8 is executed as during a walk and sitting trot except that the rider must change diagonals in the center of the figure as he changes directions so that he will be posting consistently on the horse's outside diagonal. Thus, he may begin his figure by circling to the right and posting on the left (outside) diagonal. As he returns to the center of the 8, he changes his diagonal by sitting one beat; he will now be posting on his right (outside) diagonal as he circles to the left.

If the rider reverses directions while executing a posting trot, he changes his diagonal as he changes directions—usually at the completion of the half circle. The rider must remember that he should be on his outside diagonal at all times during figure work, and can choose his diagonal accordingly.

By this time the rider should have enough balance and control of the horse that he may begin learning to execute a new equitation figure—the serpentine. As the name implies, the rider will describe a serpent. This exercise is excellent practice in precise control as well as in changing diagonals. The rider begins the figure at one end of the ring. He moves (at a walk, trot, or canter) in a straight line across the ring. Using a fence post as a guide will help the rider in executing a *straight* line. Within about ten feet of the track, he executes a half circle and moves in a straight line in the opposite direction. Within ten feet of the other side of the track, he again executes a half circle and moves in another straight line. This is continued for as long as the rider cares to unless otherwise instructed. Upon completion, the rider halts and hesitates a moment before going on.

The serpentine is executed at a walk and sitting trot until the rider completely understands the figure. He may then practice while posting. As soon as he is able to post smoothly on turns, he should concentrate on posting on the correct diagonal. The rider, of course, is to post on the outside diagonal during his turns. This will necessitate a change in the center of the straight line, after the completion of one half circle, and before the beginning of the next half circle. These changes should be evenly executed; in other words, don't change two feet from the half circle one time and ten feet from it the next time.

## BRINGING THE HORSE TO A WALK FROM A TROT

The same aids are applied as in halting except that the rider must release them when the horse comes to a walk; otherwise he will halt completely. Should the horse attempt a complete halt, the rider will use his legs. The rider must not forget to use his back strongly. When returning to a walk from a posting trot, the rider must discontinue posting so that he is able to use his back effectively as an aid.

# 5. The Canter

The canter is the third natural gait of the three-gaited horse. It is a slow, collected gallop. There are three beats to the canter. The horse begins to canter as one hind leg pushes him forward. The front leg on the same side of his body and the diagonally opposite hind leg move forward and strike the ground simultaneously. The other front leg, or "leading leg," moves forward and strikes the ground. This is followed by a period of suspension when all four feet are off the ground as the horse leaps forward. The horse lands on the hind foot which started the canter, and the sequence of leg movements repeats itself.

This gait is comfortable to sit once the rider learns to go with the thrusting forward movement. It is a tiring gait for the horse if he has to canter any length of time, but every horse loves a good canter.

## CANTER LEADS

As one observes a cantering horse, he will notice that one front leg and the hind leg on the *same side* of his body are moving out ahead of the other front and hind leg. This is a *canter lead*. The left pair of legs will "lead" the right pair of legs for the *left* canter lead. A horse should always lead with the legs toward the *inside* of a circle for balance. If he does not lead with his inside legs he may stumble, he may change his canter leads, and he will certainly feel awkward to the rider.

A riderless horse will naturally choose whichever lead suits his purpose. A horse with a rider must be told which legs to lead with

The right canter lead is correct for moving clockwise around the ring.

The left canter lead is correct for moving counter-clockwise around the ring.

as he cannot read his rider's mind; he does not know where the rider expects to travel. The aids for a canter not only tell the horse to canter, they communicate the desired lead.

## CANTER LEAD SIGNALS

Unless the horse is trained as a hunter or jumper, he should be asked to canter from a walk, especially with a beginner aboard. If the horse breaks from a trot into a canter, the canter is apt to be too fast and uncollected to be considered comfortable or in good form. However, if the horse is trained to canter from a trot as well as from a walk, and this does come in handy, he should be taken into a canter from a slow, *collected* trot. The resulting canter will also be more collected.

There are actually three different sets of aids for the canter, depending on the training of the horse:

1. The hunter is trained to respond to *diagonal* aids.

2. Most other English horses are trained to respond to *lateral* aids.

3. The Western horse is trained to respond to *lateral* aids except the method of application is a little different than that used with the English horses and will not be described here.

### LATERAL AIDS

1. Collect the horse. This is especially important for the beginner because his first attempts at canter aids may be so confusing to the horse that he is at a loss as to what to do. If the horse is sufficiently collected, he just may canter anyway.

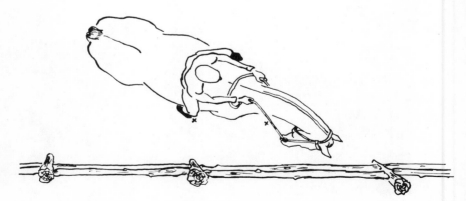

Applying the lateral aids when asking a horse to canter.

2. The rider places the horse in a diagonal position to the fence by turning the horse's head *slightly* toward the fence and using his outside leg to push the horse's rear *away* from the fence. This frees the horse's *inside* shoulder—the leading shoulder.

3. As soon as the horse is collected and positioned, the rider asks the horse to canter by shifting his weight *forward* and to the *inside* of the ring. The forward movement is executed by pushing the hips forward as when halting, and it encourages the horse to canter. Shifting the weight to the inside takes the weight off the outside hind leg—the leg which must begin the canter if one wants the inside lead.

4. *At the same time* the rider uses his outside leg behind the girth, and releases his reins just enough to give the horse's head and neck freedom to extend forward as he moves into a canter. The inside leg is used at the girth. The beginner may also reinforce his signal with another kick or two just to be certain the horse continues his canter. A school horse generally has figured out just about how many strides he must canter with a beginner before the beginner forgets to "ride" him. If the beginner gets half way around the ring the first several attempts at cantering, he should feel delighted.

5. As soon as the rider knows his horse is cantering, he must collect him, straighten his body, and set his speed so that the horse does not dash madly around the ring or through the ring. Cantering seems to be playtime for many horses. Certainly a school horse has learned most of the tricks to avoid cantering. When a horse trots, it is a steady gait; the rider may concentrate on his own position. During the canter, the rider must think about controlling the horse as well as learning position.

The object of the lateral aids is to free the horse's inside shoulder and haunch by shifting his weight to his outside legs. This is logical and effective. The only criticism is that when executing figures in an open area the rider must turn his horse *away from* his direction of travel in order to obtain the inside lead. This could confuse the horse. The rider must learn to turn the horse and signal at the same time—an act requiring a good bit of skill.

This method is called a lateral aid because the rider uses his outside rein and leg, forming a lateral line as opposed to the diagonal signals wherein the rider uses his outside leg and inside rein, forming a diagonal line.

The lateral method is the most desirable method for the beginner because he turns his horse's head to the fence, and the fence will prevent the horse from turning if the rider should over-signal him. It will also be easier for the rider to continue to maintain a slightly tigher outside rein to keep the horse on the rail.

DIAGONAL AIDS

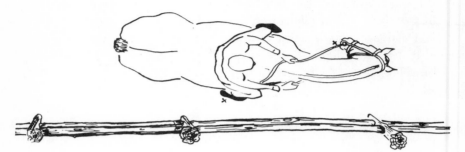

Applying the diagonal aids when asking a horse to canter.

These aids are similar to the lateral aids except the rider turns his horse's head *in the direction* of the desired lead. He uses his outside heel to tell the horse's outside hind leg to begin movement. This method is excellent when executing figures because the horse is turned in the direction of travel as he is asked to canter. The principle behind this method is that the horse knows he is to canter on his inside lead for balance, and if the rider asks for a canter while turning to the right, for instance, the horse will naturally canter on his right lead.

## HOW THE RIDER DETECTS THE CANTER LEAD

As when posting, the rider watches the shoulders of his horse. The shoulder of the leading foreleg will move out ahead of the shoulder of the non-leading foreleg. This is a little difficult for the beginner to determine because the shoulders seem to move together. The rider learns to drop his eyes to the withers and more or less look at both shoulders at the same time. The beginner may cheat a little and lean over the horse's neck. The leading foreleg will obviously move further forward than the non-leading leg. This method is hardly advocated for use except when one is first learning to detect leads, as it puts the rider in a very precarious position, gives the horse too much freedom, and looks very unsightly. The rider should strive toward the goal of "feeling" the correct canter lead. This is

The correct way to detect whether or not the horse is cantering on the desired lead. The rider has dropped her eyes, not leaned over the horse's shoulder.

The incorrect way to detect a canter lead. Rider is in a precarious position.

The incorrect way to detect a canter lead. Rider is in a precarious position.

done by the more experienced rider who will close his eyes and try to determine the lead by the position and feel of the horse's body. He can then check himself by opening his eyes and observing the lead.

If the rider discovers that the horse is on the incorrect lead, he must bring him to a walk and begin the canter again.

If the rider feels a twisting motion of his hips, the horse is probably executing a disunited canter, or cantering on one lead in front and the other lead behind. This is awkward for both horse and rider and should be corrected immediately. The horse is apt to do this if the rider signals too suddenly and scares the horse into a canter. If

Excellent position at a canter, except the reins are a bit too long for good control.

the rider turns the horse too quickly in the direction away from the legs he was leading with, the horse may have time to change his front lead for the turn, but may forget to change his hind lead also. Or perhaps the horse has kicked up his heels once or twice and changed his lead in front and not behind in the process.

## HOW TO MAINTAIN A CANTER

Occasionally one is riding a horse that does not want to continue cantering. This is especially true of the horse ridden by a beginner. The rider must learn to feel the horse slackening speed to break into a trot. The horse must not be allowed to do this. He must canter until asked to halt.

As soon as the rider feels the horse slow down, he must urge him on by using the leg on the side of his canter lead—hopefully the inside leg. The leg is used in rhythm with the horse's stride. If the horse does not respond to this, both legs may be used. The beginner will have the most difficulty in discovering just when the horse is slowing down. Usually the beginner is not aware of this until the horse is already trotting, and then it is too late. The horse should be urged back into a canter immediately, but the beginner will do better to bring the horse to a walk before asking him to canter again.

## THE RIDER'S POSITION AT THE CANTER

The slow canter is approximately the same speed as the ordinary trot. The rider's body will maintain its basic position. However, as the horse increases speed, his head and neck (and balance) will move forward, or extend, in order to obtain this speed. This will result in a forward shift of the horse's weight. The rider must also move his weight and balance forward by leaning forward *from the hips;* the back is straight and the shoulders are back.

The rider sits the canter in the same way he sits a trot with one exception. The rider's body must actively rock back and forth in a movement similar to riding a rocking horse. This rocking will offset the thrusting, leaping motion of the canter. At the same time, the rider pushes his hips down into the saddle. The rider's seat must never leave the saddle. If the horse executes a smooth canter this will not be difficult; however, the rougher the canter, the more the rider will have to work to maintain a good seat and be comfortable.

The rider must tighten his knees and thighs so that his legs will not move back and forth as the horse canters. This leg movement is not the same as the pumping motion when posting; rather the entire leg, and usually the rider's body with it, comes back as the horse seems to leap out from under the rider. The leg then moves forward as the horse seems to pick up the rider again. The rider in this case is not with his horse; he needs to tighten his entire seat as well as begin to move in rhythm with the canter.

Note rider's weak position during the canter (left lead). The hands are too high and too far forward; knees and thighs are away from the saddle; the legs are too far forward.

The rider, as when sitting the trot, must not put any more weight in the stirrups than necessary to keep his heels down and prevent a loss of stirrups; otherwise he will only push himself out of the saddle by stiffening his shock absorbers.

When the horse canters, his body seems to rock. As was mentioned before, the rider's body should rock also. The rider's hands must also move forward and back as the horse's head is lowered and raised; otherwise the horse will be continually jabbed in the mouth. This give and take will come only after the rider has learned the feel of the canter and has gained some confidence so that he may relax. Until this time, he should ride a horse that canters slowly and willingly on a loose rein.

The rider must take care not to become a passenger when the

horse canters. Do not let the horse set his own speed; the rider is to determine the speed. Any rider can cause a horse to canter fast, or gallop, but a *good* rider is able to obtain a collected canter whenever he desires. Do not let the horse play any more than can be helped. He should work at a canter in a smooth, consistent manner as he does at a trot. Do not let him decide when the canter is finished.

## REASONS FOR THE RIDER DETERMINING THE CANTER LEADS

1. The horse must canter on the inside lead in a ring in order to balance himself on turns. Try "galloping" on foot in a circle, first "leading" with your inside leg, then "leading" with your outside leg. It is much easier to turn and balance when leading with the inside leg. Think of the horse, who has *four* legs to cope with as well as a sometimes ungainly object on his back.

2. Cantering on the inside lead is required in *all* classes in the show ring.

3. The horse should be asked to change leads as the rider changes direction so that the muscles on both sides of his body are evenly developed; otherwise he will continuously canter on his preferred lead until it becomes most difficult for him to canter on the other lead.

4. To change leads on a trail rests both the horse and the rider.

## FIGURES AT A CANTER

When executing figures at a canter, the rider will learn that he must exercise a greater amount of control than when executing these same figures at a walk or trot. The horse may change speeds, especially slowing to a trot with the novice. He may speed up in order to complete the figure in a hurry. He may anticipate the rider's signals and respond before asked. He may cut the turns too short.

The rider will also discover that the figures at a canter must be larger than those executed at a walk or trot because the horse is moving faster. He will learn to maintain greater collection in order to obtain the desired responses from the horse. He will learn that his signals must be clear and precise when asking the horse to canter without a fence.

### CIRCLES

The first figure to learn at a canter is the circle. The rider will ask the horse to canter next to the rail. He will check the canter lead to be sure the horse is cantering on the inside lead. As the rider prepares to circle, he collects his horse by shortening his reins somewhat and tightening his legs. The rider should begin the circle on a turn because the horse is already bending his body and the rider, hopefully, has already shifted his weight to the inside stirrup. The rider *easily* applies direct pressure on the inside rein without easing up on the outside rein. This helps maintain an even speed and discourages the horse from trying to race around the circle. The rider must apply a minimum of pressure on the inside rein at first or the horse may turn too quickly, causing the rider to lose his balance. The bigger the circle the easier it is for the novice to execute because the horse is more apt to continue cantering, and the turns will not put the rider off balance. Tight circles are for the more advanced rider. Leg aids are used as usual for the circle.

When the circle is complete, the rider continues cantering around the ring. As soon as the rider is able to execute good circles whenever and wherever he desires with fairly good control, he is able to begin the Figure 8.

### THE FIGURE 8 AT A CANTER

It is best to learn the Figure 8 next to the rail until the rider has enough control to execute it in the center of the ring.

The rider canters around the ring on the inside lead. He *reverses* direction, executing a *large* half circle. As the rider returns to the rail, and before he has to turn the horse on to the track, he brings the horse to a walk. He should take a few steps at a walk in order to reorganize himself sufficiently to calmly ask the horse to canter on the other lead. As soon as the horse is cantering quietly and in a collected manner, the rider executes another reverse. As this half turn is complete, the rider brings the horse to a walk. He has actually accomplished a Figure 8 except one side of both circles was flat. However, having the fence as a guide facilitates learning this figure. The rider may practice it until he feels confident that he can accomplish a like figure without using the fence as a crutch. He may then try a Figure 8 in the center of the ring.

The rider halts in the middle of the ring. He must collect his horse so that he is ready and willing to canter. The rider, probably using lateral aids, will have to take great care to give a very clear signal so the horse does not become confused and fussed. The rider will use his outside rein ever so slightly; the horse will canter from the rider's use of the outside leg, shift of weight, and release of rein pressure. As soon as the horse is cantering, the rider must find which lead he is on before he begins to circle. This is asking a lot of the rider at first, but he should aim for this goal; otherwise the horse may complete half a circle before it is discovered that he is cantering on the incorrect lead. The rider must also take care to use his aids smoothly so the horse does not frantically leap forward into a wild canter.

As one circle is completed, the rider brings his horse to a walk. The rider must never be in a hurry to canter in the other direction; this will ony excite the horse and cause the figure to be executed in a somewhat less than smooth manner. The rider signals the horse when *he,* the rider, is prepared. If the horse attempts to canter before he is asked, the rider should either walk or trot around the second circle. Most horses know what the rider will ask next in figure work, and often will attempt to jump the gun. This is corrected by mixing up the figures and gaits sufficiently so that the horse must depend on his rider for commands.

As the second circle is completed, the rider halts and pauses a moment.

During figure work, if the horse should refuse to turn, the rider will apply his inside leg strongly behind the girth. At the same time he will use a give and take action on the turning rein. This will continue to remind the horse of what he has been asked to do.

A horse trained under English tack is almost always asked to come to a walk before changing leads. Advanced equitation teaches a "flying change of leads" wherein the rider signals the cantering horse to change leads without breaking gait. A Western horse changes leads automatically without breaking gait; he does not depend on his rider other than picking up his cue as the rider changes directions. This is necessary for the Western roping and cutting horses who must depend on their own tact and skill because their riders have their hands full with their cattle and cannot pay attention to details of equitation. They depend on their horses' agility and sense of self-preservation.

THE SERPENTINE

As soon as the rider is able to execute a good Figure 8, he may begin to learn the serpentine at a canter. This figure is executed as during the walk and trot except the rider must ask the horse to change leads where he would change his posting diagonals. This requires a calm rider and a collected horse. The turns may be very large at first until the rider has enough control of himself to execute these frequent changes of direction without losing his seat. The rider may also practice changing his horse's leads at the rail until he feels accomplished enough to do this away from the rail.

The rider will ask the horse to canter along the fence. As soon as the horse is cantering smoothly, the rider turns and crosses the ring. He returns to a walk as he approaches the fence, turns and walks beside the rail. Hs asks the horse to canter and turns the horse across the ring again as soon as the horse is cantering smoothly. The rider may complete the figure in this manner. When the rider is ready to practice this figure correctly, he must remember to ask the horse to canter in a calm manner and try to maintain his composure at all times.

## PROBLEMS THE RIDER FACES WHEN LEARNING TO CANTER

1. The rider must remember to "bank" on turns when cantering; otherwise it is only too easy to lose the inside stirrup, resulting in a loss of balance.

2. The rider must be careful to keep his weight out of his stirrups, although his heels must remain down. If he is leaving the saddle when the horse is cantering, the rider is probably pushing himself up by stepping hard in his stirrups. This can be corrected by cantering without stirrups.

3. The novice rider is apt to lean too far forward when cantering out of a false sense of security. This looks unsightly because the rider is usually leaning forward by rounding his back and shoulders. This should be corrected as soon as possible, before it becomes a habit.

4. The rider may be tempted to hang on to the pommel for security. This security is false, and the rider's loss of control can allow a horse to have a merry gallop.

5. The rider may lean too far back when cantering. This may result in a loose, insecure seat as the rider's legs usually end up too far

Although the rider is leaning a bit forward and not using her back as she should, she is using her legs and reins sympathetically and the horse is cooperatively backing correctly.

forward and the rider is out of balance with his horse.

6. Occasionally a rider will ask a horse to canter without shortening his reins first. The horse speeds up and the rider cannot control him. The rider must therefore take care to shorten his reins *before* he asks the horse to canter.

7. A rider may attempt to balance on the reins. If he does, the horse will not continue to canter for him.

8. If the rider jerks back on the reins as his body jerks back when the horse takes the first canter stride, he was not prepared to canter.

9. The rider should not bring his calves into the horse's sides for security. This only weakens his seat as it raises his heels and loosens the contact of his upper legs. It may also annoy the horse and cause him to speed up. After all, isn't that what tight legs mean?

# 6. Backing the Horse

The horse is asked to back from a standstill. The rider must collect his horse before asking him to back so that the horse is prepared for the signal. This is done by using hand and leg aids. The rider closes his legs to cause the horse's hindquarters to move forward, but does not allow the horse to move his front legs forward. This is particularly important if the horse is standing at a stretch. The instant the horse is on the bit, or collected, the rider begins a series of light give and take actions on the reins through the wrists and fingers. At the same time he shifts his weight down and back as if halting. His lower legs tighten. This continues until the horse has taken at least three steps back. Each step is independently asked for with a release of aids before asking for the next step. The aids are then released and the horse is promptly asked to walk forward. The rider must *never* cluck or kick the horse when backing. These are signals to go forward and will only serve to confuse the animal.

Some words of warning. The horse must back in a straight line. If he zigs, the rider must use his leg aids and possibly hands to correct this. The horse *must not* be allowed to put his head up when backing. He must not be allowed to pull his chin to his chest. These defenses signify the horse is trying to escape the action of the bit or the uncomfortable pull of the rider. The rider must be sure the horse's head is flexed (bent) at the poll and his jaw is relaxed before asking him to back. This is done by lowering the hands and using a light give and take on the bit accompanied by the other aids until the horse has relaxed his jaw and arched his neck. Only then is he ready to back correctly. Never pull straight back on the reins without releasing pressure. This will bring resistance and the horse may rear.

One cannot force a horse to back. Notice that no matter how hard the rider pulls, the horse is stubbornly refusing to budge.

Never try to make the horse back up by strength alone; the horse will win.

A horse should be taught to back simply because there are situations which may arise when the horse *has* to back up. If one has difficulty teaching the horse to back, have someone step on his front hooves as the rider signals the horse. If this does not work, a slight kick in one shin and then the other will. One or two steps at a time is plenty for the horse that is learning. The well-trained horse should be able to back indefinitely and fast enough so that it looks almost as if he were trotting.

# 7. *Adjusting the Tack*

## TO TIGHTEN THE GIRTH FROM THE SADDLE

During the course of a ride one may discover that his girth is too loose for safety. Perhaps the rider is unable to tighten the girth sufficiently from the ground because of lack of height or strength. Because of increased leverage the rider is better able to accomplish this while in the saddle. Added to this is the fact that by this time the horse has forgotten he had rebelled to the tightening of the girth and is quite relaxed.

The girth should be tightened on the left side, as it would be if the rider were working from the ground; however, if there are not enough holes in the left billet straps it is perfectly all right to tighten the girth on the right side.

The rider takes all the reins in his right hand. He *never* lets go of them. The rider leaves his *left* foot in the stirrup and brings it forward over the horse's left shoulder. The stirrup iron will dangle from the rider's toe. This is a safety precaution—should the horse act suddenly the rider can let go of the billet strap and lower his foot very quickly. He is then in a position to take command of the situation. The rider does not have to worry about the girth falling free of the billet straps because there are two or three buckles concerned, and he will only tighten one at a time, leaving the remaining one or two holding the saddle on.

From this position the rider raises the flap of the saddle and may either hold it in his right hand, still holding the reins, or slide it under his left leg. With his left hand, index finger under the billet strap, finger tips pointing toward the horse's tail, and thumb on top,

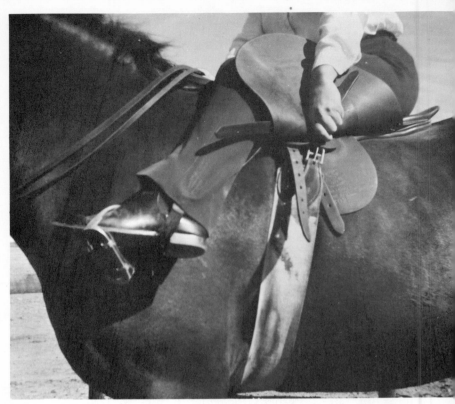

The correct way to tighten the girth while mounted.

The rider's hand is in an incorrect position for tightening the girth. She will be unable to slip the tongue of the buckle into the hole.

the rider will pull one billet strap up as high as it will go. The index finger, if correctly held, is in a position to slide the tongue of the buckle into the nearest hole of the billet strap. The rider will then adjust the other buckle or buckles accordingly. All straps must be evenly buckled or a bulge under the saddle flap will cause discomfort to the rider's legs.

This is generally done at a standstill, but in the case of an accomplished rider, may be done at a walk.

## TO ADJUST THE STIRRUPS FROM THE SADDLE

After mounting, the rider may discover that his stirrups are too long or too short even though they were measured and adjusted from the ground before mounting. As a first rate beginner, one may have his instructor adjust them; as a more accomplished rider, one must learn to do it himself.

The correct way to adjust stirrups when mounted.

The rider will remember that his stirrup irons should touch his ankle bones or a little below when his feet are out of them. The rider will make this test before deciding what adjustment to make.

The rider will leave his foot in the stirrup during the adjusting for two reasons: safety in case of an unexpected action, and so that he is better able to feel when the stirrups are adjusted comfortably and correctly.

If the rider is adjusting the left stirrup first, he puts the reins in his right hand and picks up the loose strap of the stirrup leather with his left hand. He pulls the tongue of the buckle out of the hole and will either push down with his foot to lengthen the leather or pull up the strap to shorten it. He puts the tongue of the buckle in the preferred hole. If the rider counted the holes as he was adjusting, the other stirrup leather may be easily adjusted. The rider must be sure his stirrups are even. It is awkward to ride with one leg shorter than the other, and it is uncomfortable for the horse because of the uneven weight distribution. The rider must also be certain to work the leather up so the buckle is under the saddle skirt or his leg may be rubbed.

## FLYING DISMOUNT

There are some emergencies when it is better to give up the ship than to remain on board and sink. The same applies to horseback riding: an emergency may arise when it is better to get off the horse as fast as possible for safety's sake. Thus, all riders should learn, and all instructors should teach, the flying dismount. This not only allows the rider to dismount quickly, it also lessens his fear of falling from a moving horse.

The rider learns to do this at a standstill, then at a walk, and later at a trot. It may be learned at a canter, but if the rider can do it successfully at a trot, he can also do it at a canter. The rider should also learn to do this from both the left and right sides of the horse.

An encouraging note here is that the horse will most often halt when he feels his rider's weight leave the saddle. He has been taught, or should be taught, to halt when the rider falls, and besides, without a rider he has no reason to continue onward.

To execute the flying dismount from the *left,* the rider will take the reins in one hand. He removes his feet from the stirrups. Upon the command, "Dismount," the rider vaults out of the saddle to

Flying dismount (step 3) : Rider lands facing front of hor

Flying (emergency) dismount (step 1): 1) feet out of stirrups; 2) reins in left hand.

Flying dismount (step 2): Rider vaults off horse.

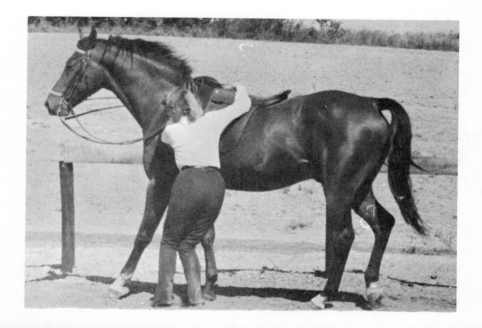

the ground. This is accomplished by placing the hands and weight on the pommel of the saddle or on the neck of the horse. The rider pushes his body up and to the left. He swings his right leg quickly over the horse's rump as he jumps to the ground. The rider should avoid scooting around the saddle on his stomach as is so often the case with first attempts at this. The exercise calls for actual vaulting.

As the rider hits the ground, he should bend his knees and ankles so that his joints are better able to absorb the shock; otherwise, his ankles will painfully receive all the concussion.

The rider will walk to his horse's head and await further instruction.

The rider should attempt to maintain contact with the reins throughout this entire exercise, but he must also be very careful not to pull them as he is vaulting off the horse.

## BUCKLES

It seems rather peculiar that equitation students should be taught the art of buckling and unbuckling, but this seems to be one of the most puzzling problems for the novice. Thus a short section on the subject may be beneficial.

A buckle is a marvelous invention for all purposes, but most particularly is it useful when attached to horse equipment. The only problem one will really encounter is when the buckle does not work as efficiently as one's belt buckle—usually the only buckle most students have encountered thus far. This problem may occur when the horse has rubbed his head thoroughly in mud or manure during a pleasant roll, and the halter buckle has become encrusted. It may occur with a new piece of equipment which has not limbered up. It may occur with stiff old leather or in the case of a bent buckle. Whatever the reason, the buckle will be most unhandy to work with.

The student may first of all attempt to unbuckle the buckle by the conventional method. If this is successful, all well and good. Chances are it will not be and the student only makes matters worse by bending and pulling the strap up higher and higher. The results will not be release of the tongue of the buckle, but a pulling of the halter itself higher and higher until the poor horse thinks he is about to be choked and the student becomes increasingly impatient.

One method the student may try is to hold the strap firmly with a slight *downward* tension. He pushes the *buckle* up and the tongue will handily slide out of the hole.

When working with an obstinate buckle the rider should pull the strap down and pull the buckle up.

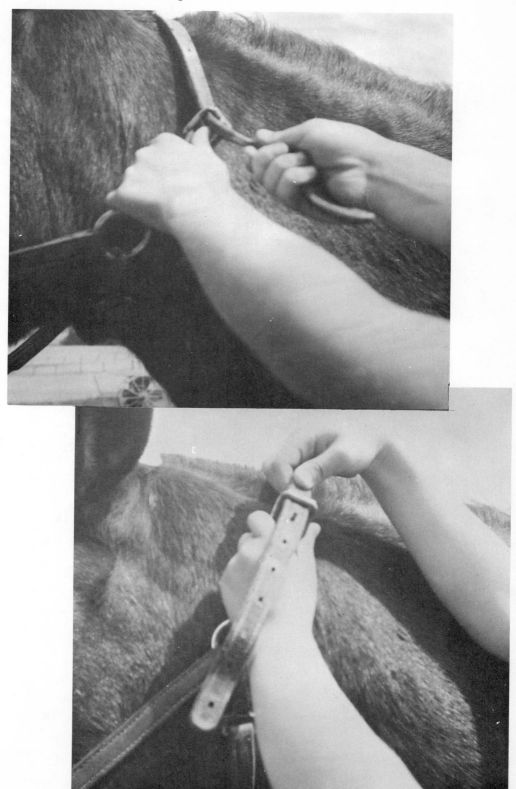

Hold buckle while attempting to push the straps down to unbuckle.

If this is unsuccessful, the student may hold the buckle firmly in one hand while pushing the strap (above the buckle) down into the buckle. The student continues pushing until the tongue is in a position parallel to the ground. He may either continue pushing until the leather strap pops off the buckle tongue, or, in extreme cases, may take a screw driver or similar object and insert it between the buckle and strap—under the loop formed by the strap as it was pushed down and not released by the buckle tongue. He is then able to work the leather off of the tongue and the two pieces are again independent.

The buckle tongue and strap should be oiled so that they will be easier to maneuver next time.

# 8. *Tacking the Horse*

## SADDLING THE HORSE

Generally the horse about to be tacked up is tied so that he is easier to manage. The saddle is put on first so that the horse may remain tied by halter and rope.

An English saddle pad is similar in shape to the underside of the saddle. It is attached to the saddle by looped straps which fit over one billet strap. A saddle pad has two very important functions. It protects the horse's back from the saddle because it absorbs moisture and eliminates the possibility of sores should the saddle have some defect. It protects the saddle from the horse's perspiration. If the rider prefers not to use a pad, as some do, he must be very sure he cleans the underside of the saddle each time it is used.

The saddle should fit the horse correctly and comfortably or chafing and pressure sores on the horse's spine may develop. The pommel of the saddle must never rest on the horse's withers; neither should the cantle rest on the spine. The saddle rests on the muscles on either side of the horse's backbone. This large padded area on the underside of the saddle will evenly distribute the weight of the saddle and rider so that the horse is comfortable.

The rider will take the saddle off the rack with the pommel over his left arm and the cantle over his right. The girth should be over the saddle or tucked up into the right stirrup iron. This keeps it out of the way when the saddle is placed on the horse's back. For the same reason the stirrup irons should be up on the leathers. The pad should be squarely under the saddle.

The horse is approached from *his* left side. The saddle is *laid*

119

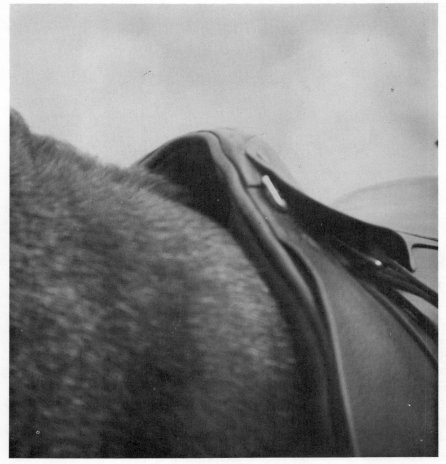

Correctly fitting saddle.

*gently* on his withers, quite a bit forward of the correct position. The rider then slides the saddle back toward the horse's tail until it "settles" in the correct place on the horse's back. This will smooth out any rumpled hairs that may otherwise irritate the horse. The pommel will be over the horse's withers.

The right side of the saddle should be checked to be sure the pad is in the correct position and there are no parts of the saddle turned under. The girth is allowed to hang down.

The rider goes back to the horse's left side and puts his right hand under the saddle *and pad* at the cantle and his left hands under the saddle and pad at the pommel. He gives a little lift to provide

The correct way to carry a saddle.

The saddle is placed further forward than the correct position so that it will smooth out any ruffled hairs as it is slid back into the correct position.

Sliding the saddle back into place on the horse's back.

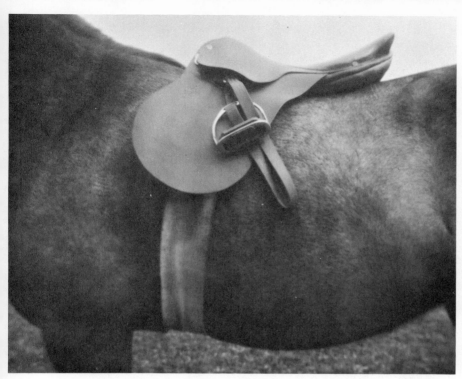

This saddle is too far back.

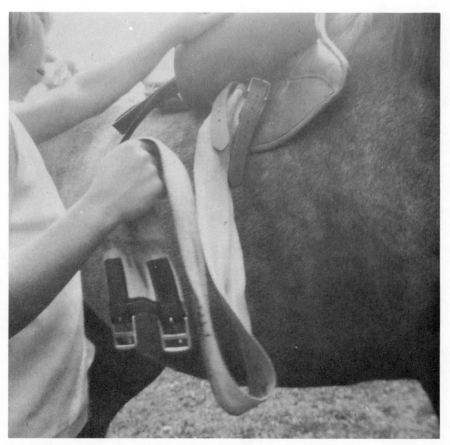

The rider goes to the horse's right side to straighten the girth and billet straps before tightening the girth.

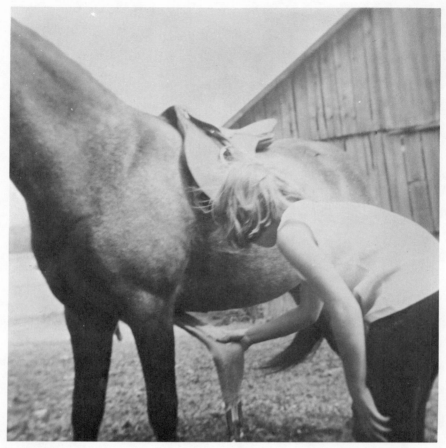

Bringing the girth under the horse's stomach in preparation for tightening it.

an air pocket along the horse's spine. This keeps the horse's back cooler and more comfortable.

The rider reaches under the horse's stomach for the girth. It is fastened to the billet straps as tightly as can be without too much effort. It may have to be tightened several times before the rider actually mounts. If the girth is tightened gradually, the horse is less apt to resent it than if the rider spends five minutes pounding or kicking the horse's stomach to make him release his gulp of air that has expanded his rib cage. This has little effect on the horse other than to make him quite angry and much harder to saddle the next time. The girth, when tightened, should be several inches behind the horse's elbow to prevent chafing. Should the horse be subject to girth sores, and some are if they haven't been ridden for a long time, a sheepskin girth cover may be used, or a string girth similar to a western cinch. The girth is tight enough if the rider

These billet straps are on each side of the saddle under the flap. The girth can be adjusted from either side.

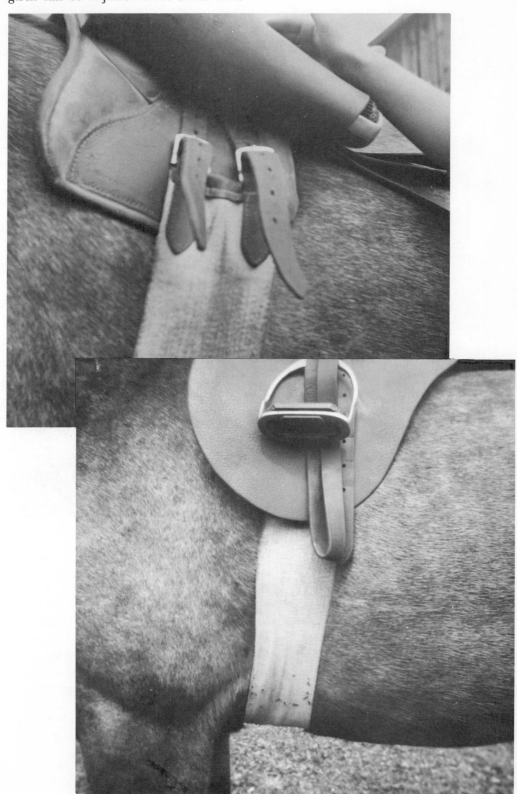

Good position of the girth—just behind the horse's elbow, but not too close as to cause irritation.

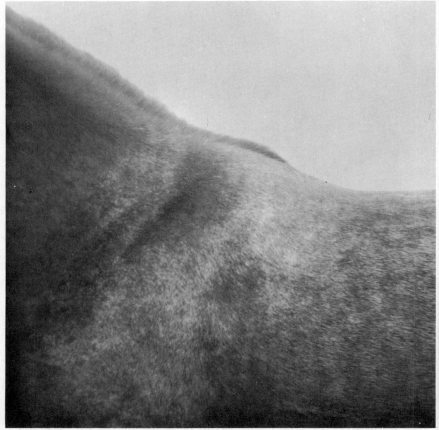

Smooth, round withers and back require a flatter saddle.

can fit his flat hand between the horse and the girth with little room
to spare. Few people can over-tighten a girth—a fear of the student
saddling the horse for the first few times. On a round-backed horse
the saddle may slip when the rider mounts regardless of how tight
the girth. The answer to this is to have an assistant give the rider a
leg up or hold the right stirrup iron tight as the rider uses the left
to mount.

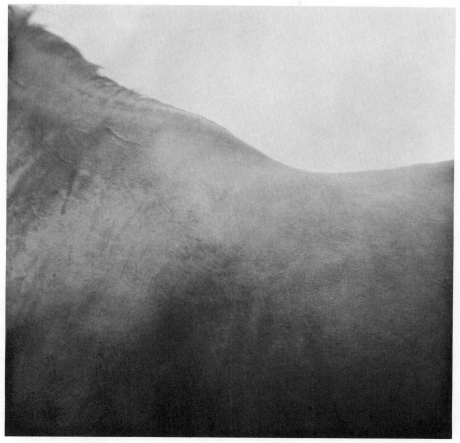

Boney withers and spine require a saddle with more padding on the underside to prevent bruising.

## BRIDLING

Before the halter is removed from the horse's head, the bridle reins are put over his head on to his neck just behind his ears. This gives the rider some control while he is bridling. The crown piece of the halter is unbuckled. The noseband of the halter is slipped down off the horse's muzzle. The crown piece is rebuckled on the

Straightening out the bridle straps and preparing to put the reins over the horse's head on to the neck is the first step in bridling.

horse's neck. This also provides added assurance that the horse cannot escape. Probably the left chain of the cross-tie will have to be unfastened and out of the rider's way.

The bridle straps should be straightened out and organized so the rider can bridle easily. The crown piece is held in the right hand, more or less hanging from one's thumb.

Putting the reins over the horse's head.

With reins on the horse's neck just behind the ears, a rider can maintain control when bridling.

Unsnapping the halter. The bridle is hanging on the right arm.

There are two methods that have proven the most satisfactory for getting the bit in the horse's mouth and the bridle on his head. The actual bridling would be very easy if the horse were a statue; however, he certainly is not and certain novice-type actions annoy him to the point where he resents being bridled and very quietly and firmly wiggles his head and clenches his teeth just enough to frustrate the novice's attempts.

To bridle the small or easy to bridle horse, the rider will hold his right hand and bridle crown between the horse's ears. This will keep the horse's head down. The bit should be placed between the horse's lips by the fingers of the rider's left hand, the fingers forward as if asking for something. The thumb is placed in such a position behind the mouthpiece of the bit so that it can be easily slipped into the corner of the horse's mouth—he has no teeth there! This bad-tasting human thumb is reason enough for the horse to open his mouth in an attempt to spit it out. This is the rider's chance to slip the bit easily between the horse's teeth and at the same time pull up on the crown piece with the right hand. The rider must never push against the horse's teeth in an attempt to force his mouth open; this will only bring about more resistance.

An alternate method is to put the right arm under the horse's

Slipping the noseband of the halter off the horse's nose.

The rider slides the halter back on the horse's neck as an added control if necessary.

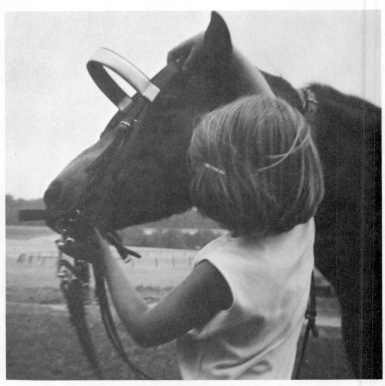

Holding the bridle and bits correctly.

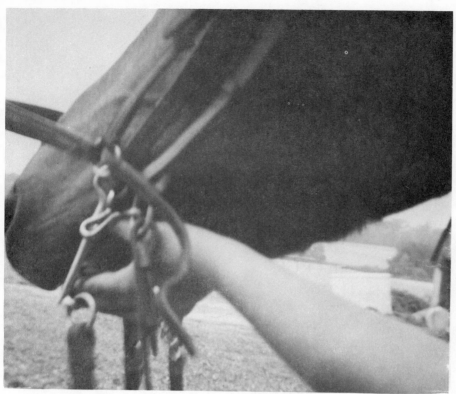

The correct way to place the bits in the horse's mouth.

The bridle has just been placed over the horse's left ear.

The bridle is on the horse's head but the necessary straps are not yet fastened.

neck and around his face where the bridle is held. The rider has more control of the horse's head.

After the bit is in the mouth, the crown piece is slipped over the horse's ears; the ears should be laid back in a natural position.

The rider must check all cheek straps to be sure they are straight. The throat latch is fastened loose enough that a clenched fist can fit between it and the horse's throat. If it is any tighter the horse may choke when he raises his head and arches his neck. The throat latch will keep the bridle on the horse's head in case the crown piece should be rubbed over the horse's ears. The cavesson is fastened next. This should be fairly tight. It is to keep the horse's mouth

The throat latch is fastened loose enough to get a fist between it and the horse's throat.

closed and prevent his moving the bit around in his mouth. The curb chain is fastened. The links must be flat or the horse will be in pain whenever the bit is used. The chain is fastened just tight enough that there is a 45 degree angle made by the horse's mouth and the shank of the bit when the bit is pulled back. Any looser and the bit has lost its effect and is a useless piece of metal hanging in the horse's mouth. Any tighter and the horse will be uncomfortable. A snaffle bit has no curb chain since it works as a nutcracker as opposed to the lever action of the curb bit and chain. In the case of a Weymouth bridle with two bits, the rider must be sure to get both bits in the horse's mouth. The curb chain is fastened behind and below the snaffle bit.

When the bridle is on the horse, the rider may do well to be

The cavesson should be tight, but a finger should be able to slip between it and the horse's jaw.

The curb chain or chin strap should be fastened tight enough for the shanks of the bit to form a 45° angle with the horse's mouth when the reins are pulled back.

The angle of the horse's mouth and the shank of the bit should be no less than a 45° angle when the reins are pulled back. This makes for a correct and comfortable fit.

sure it is of the proper fit. The curb bit should come just to the corner of the horse's lips; there should be no wrinkles. The mouthpiece should be wide enough that the horse's mouth is not pinched. The snaffle bit alone or with a curb bit is a little tighter, causing a wrinkle in the corners of the lips. If the bit hangs too low, it will cause discomfort to the horse as well as losing the effect it was designed to create. There is also the remote possibility that the bit may be low enough to actually come out of the horse's mouth. If the bit is too tight the horse will be most uncomfortable and show it.

Another item to check is the browband. Occasionally a horse with

The correct way to hold the bit when putting it in the horse's mouth.

a wide forehead will be wearing a browband that is a little too short. This will pinch his ears against the crown piece—a terrible discomfort. The browband should be of ample length. One cannot expect a horse to perform at his best when he is in pain.

If the throat latch is too tight, the rider would do well to check the browband. It may have slipped to a position low enough to take up the excess of the throat latch. The browband should be pushed up to the horse's ears.

## UNBRIDLING

Because the horse will be tied, he should be unbridled first, so that he will be tied while the rider unsaddles and grooms him. A horse must never be tied by his bridle. A bridle is too easily broken. If the rider must tie the horse with his bridle on, he can put the halter on the horse's head over the bridle or just slip it on the horse's neck.

Before the bridle is removed, there are several straps that must be unfastened: the throat latch, the cavesson, and the curb chain. If the horse has a curb *strap* (a leather strap instead of a chain) it

When unbridling, the halter should be held over the rider's arm.

While the rider is putting the halter on the horse, the bridle should be hung over her arm after its removal so as not to be stepped on.

does not have to be unfastened. The rider can remember which straps to unfasten easily because they are all at the *back* of the horse's head. Do not ever unfasten any of the cheek straps.

When the straps are unfastened, the rider slips the crown piece of the bridle over the horse's ears. He will leave the reins over the

The correct way to carry or hang up a bridle.

horse's neck until the horse is safely haltered. The bridle is allowed
to drop *slowly* down until the horse spits out the bit. It should never
be jerked out of the horse's mouth! The bridle is hung over the
right arm until the halter is on the horse. Do not drop it on the
ground where the horse could step on it.

After the halter is on, the reins are brought over the horse's head.
The bit or bits are thoroughly wiped off with a towel. The bridle
is hung up by the crown piece. If the reins hang to the floor they
should be brought up over the crown piece. Rats love to chew well-
oiled leather.

## PUTTING ON THE HALTER

The halter is the leather head stall the horse wears in the stall or pasture, although it is better to leave it hanging outside the stall unless the horse must be tied. A horse can easily get his feet tangled in one unless it fits well.

The halter is made up of a noseband, crown piece, and throat latch. It fastens on the horse in one of two ways: by a buckle at the crown piece or by a snap at the throat latch (this type of halter still has a buckle at the crown piece, but it is mainly for adjustment, as a snap is easier to manipulate) . The rider must decide which type of halter he has. He must next decide which piece is the noseband and face this forward. The horse's nose is slipped through this and the crown piece is either brought over the horse's ears and the throat latch fastened, or the crown piece is buckled behind the horse's ears. The halter should fit snugly, but not tightly enough to cause rubs or other marks. If the horse must always wear a halter, it would be considerate of his owner to put sheepskin on the crown piece and possibly on the noseband, as these two cause the greatest chafing and discomfort.

## UNSADDLING

Supposedly the rider put his stirrup irons up on the leathers when he dismounted. He should also have loosened the girth a notch or two to allow the horse's back to cool slowly as well as to allow the blood to slowly expand the veins to their normal size; otherwise, the blood might return in a sudden gush which could rupture a vessel. Because the horse is to be tied, the saddle is removed last.

The rider unbuckles the girth and lets it fall *gently* under the horse's stomach. The rider should go to the horse's right side and lay the girth over the saddle if it is clean or tuck it into the right stirrup iron if it is dirty. This keeps the girth out of the dirt and debris on the floor as well as leaving it in a position to make saddling easier the next time. The saddle is lifted off the horse's back and placed on a saddle rack, usually with the pommel facing the back of the rack. If the pad is wet, it should be allowed to hang down and dry; otherwise the pad is to remain under the saddle. If the saddle is muddy or sweaty, it should be soaped to clean it off.

## COOLING OFF THE HORSE

If the rider is cautious, he will have walked the horse long enough when coming back to the barn that he does not have to cool the horse once he has arrived. There are instances, however, when the horse is too nervous to cool off with a rider on him, or too bad mannered to walk back to the barn. In the case of a show horse, he is not allowed to relax long enough to cool out with a rider on him. A rider should never deliberately allow the horse to gallop back to the barn.

In any case, the horse must be cooled off before he is groomed and returned to his stall. There are several reasons for this: first of all, a horse could get quite stiff and cramped if allowed to stand and cool. The horse could get quite a chill. The horse could become foundered, a condition where the blood more or less settles in the feet, causing an expansion of sensitive tissues. Because the walls of the hooves are hard, they will not expand and the horse will be in great pain from the resultant pressures. This condition could cause a chronic, if not permanent, disability.

The horse should be at least breathing normally when he is brought into the barn to be untacked. If he is sweaty, the rider will untack him quickly and rub him thoroughly with a towel. A cooler or similar absorbent-type blanket is put on the horse. These are made of wool and not only prevent sudden chilling but also absorb much of the moisture. The horse is then walked, with intermittent sips of water, until he is cool *between his front legs*. The cooler is removed and the horse is thoroughly groomed.

If the weather is warm, the horse may be sponged with warm water to which a little Veterinary Absorbine has been added. The excess water is removed with a sweat scraper, a cooler is put on the horse, and the horse is walked until dry. If the weather is quite warm, the cooler may be removed after a few minutes and the horse may be walked until the excess moisture has evaporated. The horse may then graze as long as he is not subject to a chilling breeze.

A horse that is warm because of humidity rather than internal heat may be sponged off or even hosed with cold water and allowed to graze until dry. In any case, the rider must use his own judgment. His concern is not allowing the horse to become chilled, not allowing him to drink too much cold water at once, and not feeding him grain when he is over-heated.

## GROOMING THE HORSE

Grooming is one of the most important phases of horse care. It not only keeps the horse clean, it keeps him healthy. It discourages parasites, it increases circulation and relieves many itches, and it gives the owner a chance to check for injuries. Ideally, the horse should be groomed every day if he and his coat are to be kept in the best condition and health. He should be groomed before he is ridden so that he looks his best; he must always be groomed after being ridden so he feels his best.

The first grooming tool to use is the curry comb. There are actually two types of curry combs. The metal curry comb is used to remove dead hair in the spring and fall when the horse is shedding. It can be used to remove manure and dried mud. It can be used to clean out the brushes used in grooming. Because of its sharp

Rubber curry comb and dandy brush.

Grooming tools: 1) metal curry comb; 2) plastic curry comb; 3) dandy brushes; 4) body brushes.

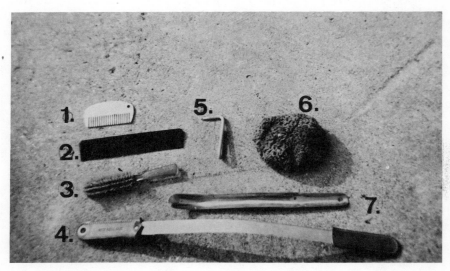

Grooming tools: 1) metal mane comb; 2) plastic mane comb; 3) old hair brush; 4) shedding blade; 5) hoof pick; 6) sponge; 7) sweat scraper.

teeth it should be used with care. The horse will tell you when the pressure is more than he can tolerate.

The rubber or plastic curry combs are similar except in material. They are used in a circular motion around and around with a good bit of elbow grease. This will loosen dirt and dead hair, massage the skin and scratch the itches. Curry combs may be used all over the horse's body except on the boney areas of the head and legs where they could bruise the delicate skin and tissues.

One begins grooming the horse behind his ear on his left side. He works from front to back. He must be sure to clean the horse's stomach, between his front legs, the insides of his back legs, and the dock of his tail. These are the most neglected areas. As one grooms the horse he continually cleans out his brushes by scraping them with the curry comb. It is impossible to get a horse clean when using dirty brushes.

The dandy brush is the grooming tool generally used after the curry comb. This is a long-bristled stiff brush that is most effective when the horse has a long winter coat or when there is quite a bit of dead hair to remove. This has little effect on a horse's sleek summer coat. The brush is used with a good deal of elbow grease in the direction of the growth of the hair. Short, quick strokes are more effective than long, lazy ones. The dandy brush is used all over the horse's body except his face. The horse does not like the discomfort of stiff bristles on his face.

The next grooming tool is the body brush. This is a brush with short, very thick, soft bristles. This brush puts a finish on the horse's coat. It is used mostly on the summer coat, as it is not too effective on a long, rough winter coat. This brush may be used on the horse's face.

The mane comb is used to comb out the mane, tail, and forelock; however, because of its tendency to tear the hairs and thus shorten the mane and tail, it should be used only on special occasions. A discarded hair brush is very good for day to day mane and tail care. For special occasions, time should be taken to pick out the mane and tail hair by hair before they are combed. This makes for a gloriously full, shiny tail, and a beautiful mane. There are special tricks to tail care, such as carefully washing the tail first, rinsing it very well, and having the finger tips coated with a little hair oil during the picking out process. Be careful not to use too much oil or the dirt will stick to the hair.

The horse's entire body, including legs and face, should be gone

Picking out a horse's tail.

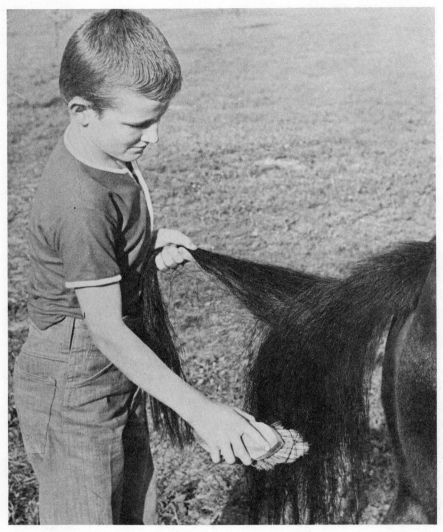

Brushing the tail after picking it out.

over with a clean towel in the direction of the hair. This picks up
any remaining lint or dandruff. The horse's eyes and nostrils may
also be wiped out with the towel.

The hoof pick is used to clean out the horse's feet. They should
be cleaned out before riding so that all manure and foreign matter
is removed and the horse's feet have a chance to air out. They should
be cleaned after riding so that the rider can check for any stones

Cleaning the hoof (step 1): shift horse's weight over to his other side.

which may have become wedged between the frog and bars of the hoof.

The horse's feet should be cleaned out in the same order each time so that he is ready to pick up each foot as the rider is ready to clean it. The rider approaches the horse's left shoulder, facing the rear. He pushes his weight against this shoulder as he brings his hand (the one next to the horse) down the horse's leg. When he reaches the fetlock joint he gives a little lift. The horse will obligingly lift his foot. If he resists, the rider must push a little harder on the horse's shoulder and lift the foot with greater firmness. The

Cleaning the hoof (step 2) : slide the hand down the leg and give a pull up on the fetlock joint.

rider pushes on the horse so that he can cause him to shift his weight on to his other foot, making it easier to lift the foot to be cleaned. The hoof is supported by holding it in the hand. The hoof is cleaned from front to back or back to front, whichever will remove the dirt the easiest. All the dirt must be removed from the frog and from between the frog and bars. This is most important as the horse could develop "thrush" in this area. Thrush is a fungus infection that can cause lameness. It can be most difficult to cure if it is allowed to work its way into the inner recesses of the foot.

Cleaning the hoof (step 3) : pick dirt and foreign material out of the hoof.

Picking up the hind foot is a similar operation except this foot will not raise as high as the front foot and is often harder to hold. The rider must be very firm about this or the horse may create problems whenever he is to have his feet handled.

When a hoof is clean it should be gently set down, never dropped.

Upon completion of the grooming process, the grooming tools are cleaned out and put away. The horse is returned to his stall. A fresh bucket of water should be available. If the horse is to be kept especially clean a stable sheet may be put on him while he is still in the cross-ties; otherwise it is unnecessary to blanket a horse unless he is ill or it is extremely cold outside.

# 9. *Emergencies*

## EMERGENCIES

Quite often a rider is faced with some type of emergency to which he has no idea how to react. This chapter is devoted to some of the most common situations in which the rider may find himself.

A horse, especially a young one, that has been left in the stall for several days will be so delighted to get out in the open again that he is apt to buck, especially when asked to canter. This usually consists of several leaps into the air and is not aimed at unseating the rider. The horse just wants to get the kinks out of his legs. This whole affair can be eliminated if the rider will let the horse loose or work him on a lunge line for a few minutes before riding him. If the horse does buck, it should be discouraged for the sake of good manners. This is done by pulling the horse's head up and moving him on. A sharp tone of voice calling his name, or anything else that comes to the rider's mind, will also serve to distract the horse from his playfulness. The rider must remember that the horse must have his head down to buck.

Rearing is one of the most dangerous habits a horse can have. If one's horse rears consistently when he cannot have his own way, he should be sold. It is too easy for the horse to lose his balance and fall back upon his rider.

The rider can tell when the horse threatens to rear. The horse is usually balking and refusing to go in a certain direction. He begins tossing his head and shifting his weight back. The rider must loosen his reins and urge the horse forward. Even if he has to let the horse have his way for a moment, it is better than letting the horse rear. The rider can easily work toward his own goal in a more subtle manner. Calling the horse's name in a firm voice and slapping the side of his neck may discourage rearing as will turning the horse's head back toward the rider's leg.

Because of the danger of rearing, the horse should not be taught this stunt because he may perform it only too easily with a clumsy-handed novice aboard. A beginner must also be sure that he has released rein pressure when the horse has come to a halt or the horse may rear to escape the continuing pressure. Many horses rear because of the rider, not because of their own orneriness.

If the horse has succeeded in rearing, the rider must lean forward and push his hands forward so that all his weight is encouraging the horse to bring his front legs down. A kick in the sides will bring the horse down quicker as well as providing the rider with added leg grip.

As soon as the horse has returned to the ground, the rider must immediately move him on. A horse can rear only from a standstill.

If the rider pulls back on a rearing horse, there may be a resultant loss of the horse's delicate balance and he will fall back, or, in the case of a horse rearing a foot or so off the ground, the rider could pull him up higher into a very precarious position.

If the horse is showing signs of stubbornness, the rider should first of all check the cause. In many cases where a novice is riding, the horse is just plain tired of being abused, however unintentionally. Or perhaps the horse is afraid of something in the road and the rider would do well to investigate this himself. In any case the rider can turn the horse from one side to the other. The resultant loss of balance will get the horse to take a step, and generally he will continue moving. The rider should use his entire body to urge the horse forward.

If the horse should lay his ears back and prepare to kick at another horse, the rider should move the horse's rear end away from his victim by turning his head *toward* the victim. The rider should call the horse's name loudly and firmly. An habitual kicker should have a red ribbon braided in his tail as a warning to other horsemen. This sign is universal and other horsemen will beware.

If one's horse threatens to run up to another horse with the intention of biting it, the rider will call the horse's name to distract him as well as turn his head away from the victim. Occasionally, school horses will attack one another out of sheer boredom and the desire to create some excitement.

If the horse should pull his head down to eat grass, the rider should

immediately pull it up again by a series of short jerks. The rider
will discover that a steady pull is useless. The rider may also use
his legs, as a moving horse cannot eat grass.

Occasionally a horse decides it would like to roll. This may be
the case when crossing a stream or a dusty field (or a riding ring)
and the horse is tired and itchy. The rider is usually given some
warning, as the horse begins to paw the ground and lower his head.
The rider should nip this in the bud at this point. The next step
the horse takes is actually buckling his legs and lowering himself.
At this point the rider can still jerk the horse to his feet. The next
step is a plop as the horse lands on the ground. The rider will do
well to dismount at this point. Most horses hesitate a few seconds
before actually flopping over and rolling. This gives the startled
rider ample time to get clear of his horse. For the benefit of discipline, however, the rider should not let the horse actually roll, but
should jerk him to his feet and remount. This also eleminates cleaning a wet or dusty saddle, bridle, and horse.

When trail riding, the rider has discovered that there are certain
objects which, harmless though they may be, seem most fearful to
the horse. The rider must first of all understand that the horse has
very limited vision and sees things only in varying shades of grays.
His vision is a bit wavering due to the irregular shape of his eye.
He has several blind spots, depending on where his head is. As he
moves his head things may all of a sudden appear from nowhere and
this is most startling. The horse is certain that a fearsome beast has
made its appearance and threatens unknown dangers. The result
will be what we call shying—the horse moves away from this object
as fast as he can, snorting all the while. He may continue moving
and turn into a runaway, or he may just move far enough away to
feel safe. The rider should keep his horse's head turned toward the
object so that he is less apt to really bolt. Let him look carefully
at the object and even sniff it if he has enough courage to do so.
It may be well for the rider to dismount and lead the horse up to
the object to thoroughly investigate it so that he will lose his fear of
it. For some reason a horse is more willing to approach an object
when being led than when mounted. Perhaps he sees that the one
leading him has not been harmed and thus develops more confidence
himself.

Should the horse actually bolt away in fright, a sharp tug on the
reins should halt him, especially if he has left companions behind.
However, if the horse continues to run, the rider must be certain

he himself is not the actual cause. Are his heels digging into the horse's sides, encouraging him on? Are the reins waving in the wind while the rider hangs onto the saddle for dear life? The rider can just let the horse run until he is tired or he comes to the barn. He could try turning him in circles that become increasingly smaller and smaller until the horse is under control. Or he could turn him toward a solid object such as a barn wall. Few horses will run into a wall. Of course, the resultant sliding halt could unseat a rider. Whatever method the rider uses, he must remember that a steady pull will get him nowhere. Sharp tugs or a see-saw action on the horse's mouth are apt to bring a good response.

In the stall or when being groomed in the cross-ties, if the horse should attempt to bite or kick, he should be slapped on the neck or rump and his name should be called loudly and firmly. A horse must never be allowed aggressive action toward a person, as it may become a habit.

If the saddle slips slightly when the rider is mounting, he can easily complete the mounting procedure, then straighten the saddle by weighting the right stirrup. The saddle is straight when the center of the pommel is in line with the horse's withers. If the saddle slips completely to the side, the rider must remove his left foot from the stirrup immediately and jump to the ground. The girth will have to be unbuckled and the saddle replaced and tightened again. If the rider has tightened the girth before mounting and mounted correctly with his left hand on the pommel, he should not be faced with this problem.

If the rider is cantering and happens to lose his stirrups, something that often happens with a novice, he must remember not to panic. Panic stiffens the muscles which in turn may cause loss of balance. The rider must try to quietly regain his stirrup or stirrups. If this is not possible, he should bring the horse to a walk to regain them.

Occasionally when one is mounting he puts his leg in such a position as to release the safety catch on the saddle. The stirrup leather pulls away from the saddle and the rider can hardly believe it. He will have to remember not to put his left leg so high in the air the next time he mounts! Also, the stirrup leather may come off while one is mounted. A tree limb may hook onto the leather and pull it off, or the horse may have bucked, causing the rider to throw his legs up and behind him. The rider will dismount and replace his stirrup leather. He must remember to keep his heels down when the horse bucks and to keep some distance between himself and branches.

A loose horse also presents a problem. If the rider has dismounted or fallen and the horse has walked off, the rider must decide the best way to catch him or he may be walking home. Chasing a horse is an invitation to play. If another horse and rider are in the area, the homeward bound animal will usually wait for his companion, in which case his own rider can usually walk right up to him, especially if he has a handful of grass. If the unmounted horse and rider are alone, the rider must move in front of the horse and loudly say "Whoa." This may or may not work, depending on the horse and his eagerness to reach the barn. In pasture or if the horse has gotten out of the barn, a bucket with a small amount of oats in the bottom to rattle will attract the horse's attention. If he thinks food is available, he will readily come up to the one holding the bucket. Be sure the horse is rewarded or the next time he won't be so easy to catch. A horse will learn to come when called if rewarded each time with a treat or his dinner.

# 10.  General Care of the Horse

## GENERAL CARE OF THE HORSE

There are some excellent books written regarding complete care
of the horse. Only a brief guide will be given here so that the student
will at least have a general idea of how a horse is taken care of, and
perhaps he may be given the chance to care for a horse himself.

## FEEDING THE HORSE

A horse should be fed grain at least twice a day, preferably three
times. The horse has a very small stomach and very long intestinal
tract in comparison with other animals. Large amounts of grain
taken in at one time may cause colic or founder from over-eating.
Small amounts of grain fed more often result in maximum nutri-
tion, as the horse has time to digest his food properly. Hay should
be fed twice a day with the greater part at night. There is an old
theory that hay should be fed first, then water, followed by grain.
Supposedly the horse will eat his grain slower if his appetite is
slightly diminished from eating some hay beforehand. Water should
be fed before grain, the theory being that large amounts of water
following grain may cause the grain to swell, resulting in digestive
disturbances. The water also has the tendency to wash the grain
through the digestive system before all the nutrients are absorbed
from it. This theory has neither been proved nor disproved. It is
logical.

Another basic principle to follow applies to changing the horse's
diet. This must be done gradually. A rapid change is too much of

a shock to the horse's digestive system and colic may result. If one decides to feed the horse corn, he is given a little corn the first day and the amount of the other grain is decreased (if the corn is to replace the other grain). The next day feed a little more corn and so on until the change is made.

Grains are protein-type concentrates that are fed in a grain box or tub. A removable one is preferable as it can be washed out occasionally.

Oats are the safest and best grain for horses, as they are easily digested and quite palatable. They contain the most protein of all grains suitable for horses. They can be fed rolled, crushed, or whole. Oats should be clean and free from dust and rat manure. They should feel heavy. A horse should be fed about one pound of oats per 100 pounds of body weight each day. This is divided into two, preferably three, feedings. An idle horse will get less; a working horse may need more. This will depend on the horse's condition and how easy or difficult it is for him to maintain his weight.

Corn should be fed on the cob or crushed so the horse will eat it slowly, making it more digestible. It is low in protein and mineral content, but rich in carbohydrates and therefore more heat-producing than oats. Heat-producing grains also produce greater energy in the horse. They are good for fattening a thin animal. Corn is good to use in winter because of its heat-producing properties which help the horse maintain his body temperature. Because it is more fattening than oats, about three-fourths of a pound per 100 pounds of horse is fed a day. Corn must be well dried and not moldy before it is fed to a horse or it could cause digestive disturbances. It should not be fed in the summer, as it may make the horse sweat too much, resulting in a loss of weight.

Commercial horse feed is a general mixture of everything the manufacturer believes a horse should have for a balanced diet, plus molasses for palatability. It costs about twice as much as oats and corn and is not considered necessary if the horse is receiving the necessary nutrients as well as various supplements (mentioned later). It is good to feed to young, growing animals and mares in foal to be sure they are getting all the nutrients for good growth and bone development.

Wheat bran is wheat chaff ground into flakes. It is used mostly because of its laxative effect. Mares, before and after foaling, should have some in their feed each day to prevent constipation. A bran mash is unnecessary. Wheat itself should never be fed to a horse because it has too much energy intake for his system.

Barley may be fed in areas where it is abundant; however, it usually has to be soaked in water before feeding because of its hard shell, and it has no properties that cannot be derived from oats or corn.

Horses should thus be fed oats as their basic grain, with corn added for energy, additional weight, or in winter for maintaining body temperature.

Hay should be fed on the ground (not in that manure, please!) or in a low (no lower than shoulder height) manger. An overhead manger is not recommended because the horse is liable to get chaff in his eyes.

Ten to twelve pounds of hay a day, divided into two feedings with the greater part at night, is plenty for the average size horse. Too much hay will eventually result in an unsightly "grass" or "hay" belly. A horse at work should receive less hay and more grain; an idle horse should have more hay and less grain. Again, the amount is determined by the condition of the horse and the amount of work he is required to do. Hay provides the necessary bulk in the horse's diet. A horse in his natural environment eats no grain, only grass. He eats almost all the time because of his small stomach. The grass passes to the intestines almost as fast as the horse eats it. A horse, by nature, likes to munch most of the time. Just because he appears hungry because he may be eating his bedding, don't believe it. He's just following an instinctive desire. And hay must be good hay or there will be no nutritive value derived.

Timothy hay with a little clover and alfalfa is usually considered the best horse hay. The leaves should be broad and green. There should be no dust or mold to cause coughs, heaves, or colic. Mold is a whitish-green powder-type fungus growth which develops if the hay is allowed to get wet while it is being baled or when it is already baled. The hay should not give the appearance of being stemy or tough. This can be seen in hay baled too late. Besides being unpalatable, it usually means the hay lacks some of the necessary vitamins which it would normally contain if baled at the right time— just as it is ripening.

Alfalfa hay alone is generally considered too rich and laxative for horses, although a little included in your horse's diet would be welcome because it is very tasty and supplies plenty of protein, vitamins, and minerals.

New hay of any variety is very laxative and should be fed sparingly until the horse's system has adjusted to it. It is excellent for horses as it is rich in Vitamin A, and not as much has to be fed per day, as opposed to older hay which has lost some of its nutritive value.

Grass is the horse's natural food and he should have access to it whenever possible. In the early spring the grass is usually very full of water. Too much at one time may cause digestive disturbances. The best procedure to follow is to allow the horse to graze about an hour the first day. Increase the grazing time until the horse's system has adjusted to the grass; then he may have all he wants. If the horse is stabled at this time, he may have grain, but hay is not necessary as long as the grass in the pasture is sufficient. A young animal should be allowed to be in pasture for the first few years of its life. Not only does grass contain many of the nutrients necessary for growth and development, but being free to move about at will, the foal will develop good bone and muscle. Grain should be included in the diet of a young horse in pasture to stimulate growth. A mature horse in pasture should have grain if he is being ridden, but otherwise grass is sufficient.

Salt is very necessary to the horse. Without it he can barely maintain his body functions. A small block in a separate container should be in the horse's stall so he can have all he wants whenever he wants it. The trace mineral (red) salt blocks are the best, as they contain traces of all the minerals necessary to the horse. The white blocks are iodized and the blue blocks contain iron.

Water is also essential to the horse. It aids digestion, carries off body wastes, flushes out the system, and cools the animal. It should be available at all times except when the horse is overheated, then he should be allowed to have sips from time to time as he is cooling out. The water bucket should be filled (after being carefully rinsed out) several times a day, depending on the weather. The bucket can be hung in the stall on a blunt hook or, better yet, a snap. A bucket that is unfastened will surely be turned over.

Linseed Oil Meal and Soybean Oil Meal are important protein supplements. The Soybean Oil Meal contains more protein and is cheaper, so is the better buy. A handful of either in the grain twice a day will help the horse shed out his coat. It will also aid in producing a glossy coat, so is necessary in the diet when preparing a horse for show.

Carrots and apples are a delightful treat as well as a source of necessary vitamins. Sugar is unnecessary and can be detrimental.

Steamed Bone Meal provides calcium and is especially important for growing horses and mares in foal.

A horse can live easily on grass and hay alone; however, if he is to maintain any kind of good condition at all, he must also have grain. Grass and hay keep the horse's stomach fat, while grain fills out the top. The protein in grain aids in muscle development; carbohydrates produce energy and vigor. Grain is necessary for obtaining and maintaining a good condition which will make the horse suitable for any type of work. A horse cannot be considered to be in good condition (other than *looking* fat) if he is fed no grain. He will have soft, flabby muscles and little energy.

## WORMING THE HORSE

There are about 150 different equine parasites, including worms. A horse harbors some of these worms almost all of his life. They infect most areas of the horse's body including his blood stream, heart, and liver. The very wormy horse appears bloated, his eyes and hair are dull, and his skin is dry and tight. The conscientious horse owner will want to be certain that his horse is as free of these as he can be. Worms can be controlled and in some cases, with careful management, prevented. This prevention depends on the life cycle of the worm. Most worms spend the greater part of their life going through the horse. When they leave the horse, by way of the droppings, they lay eggs that are picked up (especially in pasture) by another horse and the cycle repeats itself. Pasture rotation helps to keep the worms from building up in pasture. It should be rotated every two or three weeks. Manure should not be spread in a pasture, but any that is will contain worms, so the horses must be kept out of that pasture for several weeks. Young stock and mares with colts should be pastured in a clean pasture, since worms are very detrimental to colts.

There are four main types of worms which are the most common. They will be briefly mentioned here. The bot is probably the most common and the most obvious because of the little bead-like yellow dots evident on the horse's legs in the late summer and fall. These are relatively harmless compared to the other three types. These yellow "eggs" cause an itch which the horse scratches with his nose. The eggs are then taken into his mouth where they hatch and remain in the larva stage. They are then passed to the stomach where they attach themselves and live for eight to twelve months. In the spring the larva are passed out in the horse's droppings. They spend three to five weeks on the ground in the pupa stage, then hatch into adult flies to start the cycle over again. It is important to break the life cycle of these worms while they are in the horse's stomach. The time to worm for bots is in January or late December after the first good frost. The adult Bot Flies are dead by this time and cannot lay any more eggs.

Bots can cause a loss of blood as well as breaks in the stomach lining which in turn cause colic. By weakening the stomach in this manner, bots make it possible for bacteria to take over, which may result in various infections.

The Bot fly looks similar to a gray and black bee. It whirrs around the horse's legs trying to lay eggs. For some reason the horse senses this and the result of it, for he will usually stamp his feet and act very upset. Because Bot Flies move in a jerky manner, they are hard to kill. They never actually land on the horse to lay their eggs, but lay them while they are hovering.

Round worms grow to maturity in the small intestine after passing through almost every vital organ. The damage is done enroute to the intestines. Their life cycle can be broken at any time except during the egg stage when they are encased in hard shells.

Strongyles or Blood Worms frequently cause, or indirectly cause, death, especially in younger animals. The worms are picked up in pasture as larva. They go to the stomach, small intestine, secum and colon where they penetrate the linings and get into the blood stream. The most damage is done to the aorta; the worms cause clots which weaken the walls of this main artery. Often the artery will rupture, causing death. They have also been known to get into the heart valves, again resulting in death.

The Pin Worms do not cause much damage except to the appearance of the horse's tail, which he rubs when infected. The worms live near the rectum where a good bit of irritation is caused. They cannot be detected except when they pass out in the droppings or when a horse continuously rubs his tail. (Be sure the dock of the horse's tail is not dirty or this may cause an irritation also.)

The conscientious horse owner should worm his horse three times a year, especially if the animal is in contact with other horses. Treating for worms after the first good frost will usually eliminate most of the bots. Horses should be wormed again in the spring before being pastured, and again in July or August. Before worming, a veterinarian should have a fairly fresh sample of the horse's droppings. From this he can make an egg count to determine how many and what kind of worms (except Pin Worms) the horse is infected with. He can prescribe for him accordingly. One should never attempt to worm the horse without consulting a veterinarian. Worm medicine is a poison which could result in the loss of the horse if not correctly prescribed.

## CARE OF THE HORSE'S TEETH

As the horse grows older, his teeth grow longer. He wears down part of the edges of the molars (back teeth) when chewing; however, he does not wear the entire surface down. This leaves sharp, pointed edges which irritate the gums when the horse chews. He cannot chew well and thus does not derive the maximum benefit from his food. At least once a year a veterinarian should examine the horse's mouth for teeth that need to be "dressed" or "floated." He will put a "speculum" in the horse's mouth so that he may examine the teeth easily. A speculum is a metal contraption attached to a halter. It slips into the horse's mouth and encircles his front teeth. This is cranked open, causing the horse's mouth to open and maintain that position. If there are sharp, irritating edges on the teeth, the veterinarian will take a large file, called a float, and file these edges down. The horse will be able to eat better as a result, and will stay in better condition with less food.

One sign that the horse is having difficulty chewing is the position of the head when eating. An irritating tooth will often cause the horse to cock his head. The horse may lose a lot of food out of his mouth, or there may be unchewed grain in his droppings.

## CONSTRUCTION OF STALLS

A box stall should be about 12 feet by 12 feet for the average size horse. A tie stall should be about 5 feet by 7 feet. All doors should have an 8-foot clearance and a 4-foot width. Ceilings should be 10 feet high. A horse dearly loves a window to look out of. It should be of a type similar to a dutch door so that it may be opened and shut as the weather dictates. The stall should be well ventilated but not drafty. A horse can stand cold, cold weather, but a draft could easily cause a respiratory disease.

The floor should be gravel with a layer of blue clay, over which is a layer of stone-free dirt. This type of floor allows for good drainage. Wood floors rot and cement floors are too hard on the horse's legs to be suitable.

There should be a feeding corner with a feed box, a manger, and the water bucket. The hay may be fed on the ground near the feed box if a manger is not desired. A word of warning concerning a manger—it must be high enough so the horse does not climb into it in a moment of excitement. A little over the horse's chest height is a good standard of measure.

There should be no protruding objects or nails that could hurt the horse. All buckets should be hung on blunt hooks or snaps. There should be no sharp edges where the metal of the bucket is torn.

## CLEANING STALLS

A stall should be picked out, preferably, once a day—never less than once a week. In the winter the stalls can go a little longer because of the lack of humidity which holds the moisture. If the stalls are not cleaned out every day, fresh bedding should at least be added.

To clean out a stall, first separate the good, reusable straw from the manure and wet straw. The reusable straw can be tossed into a clean corner; the dirty straw and manure are thrown into a wheelbarrow to be dumped. The stall should be raked and sprinkled with lime. This slaked lime helps to dry out the stall as well as to sweeten the stable aroma. Spread out the old, reusable straw. Add fresh bedding. Be sure it is shaken out well. Never be stingy with bedding because it is easier to clean the stall that is well bedded than it is to clean one with just a little bedding. The latter will usually require removing all the straw, while the former results in removing mostly just manure.

The fresh straw should be spread thickly in the center and thinner around the edges. A horse lies down in the center of his stall so lush bedding will be welcome. He also pushes straw to the edge of his stall as he rolls, so he may as well do this work.

The manure pile should be located somewhere behind the barn out of sight and smell. The further away it is the better, as it attracts flies. A manure spreader is most efficient.

Straw should be bright yellow in appearance. Any darker color indicates that the straw has been wet and is apt to be moldy or hard to spread. Never use moldy straw, as some horses eat their bedding.

Wheat or oat straw seems to be the most absorbent, a most desirable quality, although some horses will eat oat straw. There should be no grass or hay mixed in the straw, as this again encourages the horse to eat his bedding.

Some horses must be taken out of their stalls during the cleaning, as they insist on being in the way or resent the imposition of being moved around the stall. This is especially true in a standing (tie) stall. If the stall is particularly small the horse must be removed in order for the owner to do a thorough job of cleaning. While the horse is out of his stall, and after the stall is cleaned, the horse may be groomed. The feet should particularly be cleaned out before the horse is returned to a clean stall. If the horse is put in the pasture, the stall does not have to be bedded until the horse is to be put into it. This will hasten the drying out process.

## EXERCISE

A horse should have exercise at least once a day unless he is disabled. Even five minutes a day is better than nothing and will add some spice to the idle horse's life. One way to exercise the horse, other than riding and driving, is working him on a lunge line. This is a good way to supple the horse as well as teach him various verbal commands useful to a rider. It will also allow the horse to kick up his heels a bit.

The lunge line should be about 30 feet long and of a canvas or nylon material which will not cause a rope burn in case the horse becomes entangled. The line is attached to the halter as a lead rope would be. The trainer (I will call him this as he cannot be called the rider and may not be the owner) stands beside the horse's shoulder with the lunge line looped in his left hand if the horse is to go counter-clockwise, and in his right hand if the horse is to go clockwise. A whip should be held in the other hand. The whip hand is to drive the horse forward while the other hand leads the horse into motion. The whip will also keep the horse out into the circle, instead of rushing into the trainer. Thus the position formed by horse, trainer, and accessories forms a triangle, with the horse as one point, the whip as another, and the trainer as another. The trainer may be only a few feet from the horse. He asks the horse to move by clucking and saying "Walk." A crack of the whip may reinforce the command. The trainer may just let the horse work at will *in both directions* until he seems ready to return to the barn,

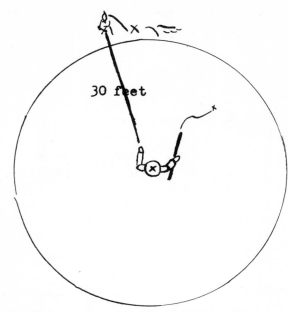

30 feet

Working a horse on a lunge line.

or he may do some educating as to the walk, trot, and canter on command. We are assuming that the horse knows and obeys the command, "Whoa." If not, he may be halted by a continual shortening of the lunge line in a manner similar to reeling in a fish. I will not delve into this phase as this is not a book on training. However, it is important and worthy of study.

The horse may be exercised in a pasture or paddock if the weather is suitable. The horse may be led about and allowed to graze a bit. If the horse is ill and unable to receive exercise in some form, a good grooming will massage his cramped muscles and make him feel so much better.

## CARE OF THE HORSE'S FEET

There is an old saying, "no foot, no horse," and it is only too true, for without the use of four legs, the horse is worthless to use. There have been a good many horses ruined or disabled by unknowing owners who provided little or no care for their horse's feet.

Stalls must be kept clean and dry to prevent thrush, a fungus infection which infects the frogs of the horse's feet. It is usually caused by the horse's standing with his feet in manure for long periods of

The toe of this hoof is overgrown and needs trimming. If the horse continues to be ridden in this condition, he may strain his tendons.

A ragged hoof which needs trimming.

Nicely trimmed hoofs.

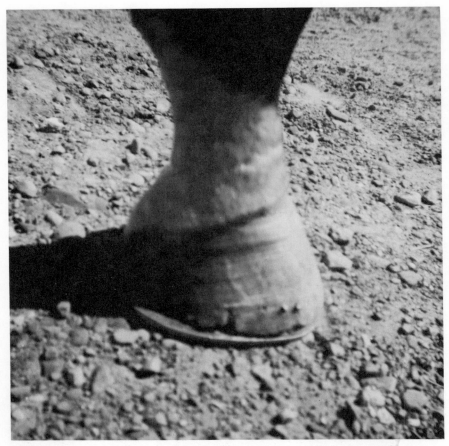

The shoe is about to come off the hoof. Notice the jagged hoof wall torn by clinched nails pulling out.

time, especially in the winter. Thrush can be detected while the hoof is being cleaned. The frog appears to be slightly rotten and there is a putrid stench along with a black discharge. A few days of the proper treatment will clear up this condition. A veterinarian should be consulted. The horse should wear shoes if he is ridden on hard surfaces; otherwise the horny wall of his hoof will wear down, allowing too much pressure on the sensitive sole and frog. The horse will then be lame. Borium on the toe and heel of the shoes will prevent the horse's slipping on paved roads. The feet should be trimmed every six to eight weeks, depending on how fast the individual horse's feet grow. If the horse is wearing shoes, they can be reset unless they are worn too much, in which case new ones will have to be made. A horse should be allowed to go barefooted whenever he is idle. This is natural for the horse and his feet will stay in better condition and health. It may also correct faults or problems that originated from shoeing.

Moisture, which is essential to the normal growth of the horn of the hoofs, is supplied by mud and water. When the horse is stabled the blood does not furnish enough moisture to keep the horn structure in perfect condition. The hoof must then be protected from wearing away faster than it grows. Therefore, it is necessary to provide shoes for this protection. The purpose of normal shoeing is to

A blacksmith filing the rough edges of the toe.

keep the hoof from breaking or wearing away too rapidly without interference with the physiological function of its structure. The purpose of corrective shoeing is to overcome faults that may arise from acquired unsoundnesses or faults in the gaits. Consistently faulty shoeing can bring on unsoundnesses to the hoof and legs and it can cause faults in the gaits.

It is very important that a good blacksmith do the shoeing. A bad job of shoeing can ruin a hoof, bow a tendon, cause corns and twisted bones, and can start such diseases as ringbone and navicular. Because a horse cannot tell the owner when a shoe hurts, the damage is usually done when the horse goes lame.

The forging and fitting of a horseshoe is a fine art. The blacksmith must have a great knowledge of the horse's feet, legs, and anatomy

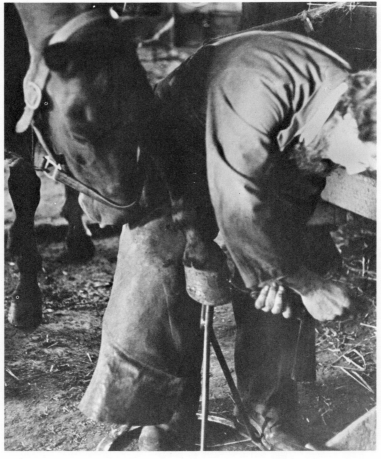

A blacksmith clinching nails as he completes the shoeing process. Note the horse's interest in the project.

as well as how to shape and fit a shoe. A good blacksmith can correct defects and peculiarities in the way the horse moves. A disreputable blacksmith can cause untold damage.

Along with keeping the horse well shod, keeping the feet and stall clean, or leaving the horse barefooted in pasture goes sensible riding. Hard surfaces plus steel shoes are not too good for the legs of the horse when ridden at faster gaits. Besides the possibility of the horse slipping and falling, trotting or cantering on paved surfaces results in a tremendous amount of concussion to the bones of the feet and legs. They cannot endure this for very long without damage, often permanent. So reserve the wild gallops for open fields where little damage, other than falling in a ground hog hole, can result.

If there is any swelling around the horse's fetlocks or tendons be extra careful, as this is a sure sign that concussion is taking its toll. The only exception in this case is with a working animal (one used to a good bit of riding) who has had to stand several days without exercise. The legs of such horses "stock up" or fill with fluid. A little exercise will reduce the swelling. Just be certain that the fault does not lie with the rider.

# 11. Care of the Tack

Because of the expense of riding equipment, it should be well cared for to ensure its long life. Ideally the bridle and saddle should be soaped each time they are used. This is not always possible. They should at least be soaped every time they begin to look dirty. Glycerine soap seems to do the best job. Cold water should be used as hot water draws out the oil and dries the leather. The sponge is dampened, the less water the better. From this point on, except when rinsing out the sponge, dip the soap in the water. This minimizes the amount of water in the sponge. The leather straps are rubbed thoroughly with the soaped sponge. The bits and metal parts are scrubbed with an S.O.S. pad, rinsed, and dried. Every so often the tack should be completely taken apart (notations made as to where the buckles buckled) and soaped with particular care for the parts which attach to the bit. These become wet from the horse's saliva and are apt to show wear easily. If the leather gives the appearance of being dry, Neatsfoot Oil is applied. It should not, however, be applied to the seat of the saddle unless the rider plans to wear old riding pants for a time or two after oiling.

New leather should be oiled before being used. It should be oiled very well on parts that will have to take a lot of wear; otherwise the leather may crack and weaken. A paint brush is an efficient means of applying oil to a saddle.

Saddle soap not only keeps the leather clean and presentable, it keeps it in a softened condition that minimizes wear. It is most important to keep the horse's halter clean, an item only too often neglected. Because the horse wears this the most and it is subject to mud and dust as the horse rolls, it becomes very dry and dirty and will cause chafing.

If the saddle must be put on the ground, it should stand on the pommel as a protection to the saddle tree and to eliminate the chance of debris clinging to the saddle pad.

A leather girth must also be kept clean for the same reason. A web girth, especially one with no leather, may be thrown into the washing machine when it is too dirty to clean in any other way. The leather suffers somewhat from this, but not appreciably. Saddle pads should be brushed frequently and washed about once a year, usually after the horse has shed out. They may be sent to the cleaners or washed in the machine using a cold water detergent. They should not be put in the dryer unless there is an air setting.

Tack should not be allowed to drag in the dirt and should be hung properly to ensure long life. The saddle, if put on the ground, should rest pommel down, cantle up. It should not be allowed to get into a position where it is apt to be scratched or the tree broken. For the same reason, the saddle should not be used as a chair.

# 12. Rules

## STABLE RULES

It is extremely annoying, and certainly rude, for strangers to wander around a stable, whether public or private, without the owner's permission. Many people feel that a barn, because it may not be locked, is a public place open to the world. The owner of a stable is very willing to welcome people with open arms and show them every horse in the barn if the visitors will seek him out and not take it upon themselves to do their own investigating.

Once one is being given the grand tour, he must make certain he conducts himself in a manner that will make him welcome again. Such standards of conduct are listed below, and the courteous horse lover will be sure he abides by them.

1. Do not smoke in a barn except in a designated area. This is a very obvious rule because of all the flammable material which a barn contains.

2. Speak in a normal tone of voice. Shouting is annoying to many horses and has no place in a barn.

3. Do not run in a barn. Again, this excites and annoys the horses.

4. Be relaxed and natural around horses. If one has never come into previous contact with horses, he may be nervous and jumpy, prone to let out horrible shrieks whenever a horse's nose comes within two feet of him. This frightens the horse, and his jumping back in turn also frightens the novice. Remember to act as natural as if the horse were just a big dog, and the relaxed, friendly attitude of the horse will be reassuring. The owner of a mean horse will always warn visitors, as will the horse's flat back ears.

174

5. Let the horse know you are approaching his stall by speaking quietly to him. If he suddenly sees someone standing there unexpectedly, it may startle him frightfully. A warning is certainly welcome to him as well as being a safety precaution for the one approaching, especially if he is approaching the horse from the rear. Many people have been accidentally kicked by a horse frightened in just this way; even the most gentle horse will utilize his heels if he considers it a matter of self-preservation.

6. Always walk around the front of the horse whenever possible. The front of the horse is generally considered safer than the rear for obvious reasons. Even the most gentle horse may be kicking at a fly, and if someone is in the way, well—! When one does walk around the rear of the horse, he should walk as close to it as possible, keeping his hand on the horse's rump. The closer one is, in case the horse kicks, the less painful is the kick because the horse has been unable to utilize the full power of the swing. Or, walk as far away from the rear as possible, completely out of range of the hind legs in case they are activated.

7. Never enter a stall or take a horse out without permission, unless, of course, you own the animal.

8. Do not feed a horse without permission. Many people do not want their horses fed by hand as it makes them nippy, or perhaps they do not want their horses to have the treat offered.

9. Small children should be kept firmly in hand. There are many potential dangers around a barn of which many people are unaware, as well as many things for a youngster to get into. The stable owner does not appreciate picking up after such a youngster once he has gone home.

## RING RULES

Ring rules are the standards by which a rider conducts himself when riding in company in a riding ring, whether showing or during instruction. A well-mannered rider is aware that their constant practice is a safety factor for others in the ring.

1. When under an instructor's supervision, it is important to obey that instructor at all times. The instructor can see potential danger and eliminate it before a student is even aware of what is going on. The instructor knows his horses so well that he can almost anticipate their actions. Thus, when an instructor gives a seemingly

senseless command, the student should obey without question. An explanation from the instructor will generally follow.

2. Always keep at least a two horses' distance between horses. This will eliminate any fighting that might otherwise develop.

3. Always go in the same direction as others unless otherwise directed. This eliminates confusion.

4. Always ride your own horse; do not tell others what to do. This is annoying to everyone concerned. The instructor is aware of what is happening, and if he feels a correction is required, he will follow through.

5. Everyone should come to a complete halt if a rider should fall off. This will calm the loose horse, making him easier to catch, and will eliminate the danger of another horse's stepping on the fallen rider.

6. The horse should be walked the first ten minutes to warm him up, and the last ten minutes to cool him out.

7. Always walk the horse in the ring unless otherwise instructed when under an instructor's supervision.

8. Let another rider know when you are approaching and preparing to pass. This will enable him to be prepared to control his horse in case of speeding up or kicking.

9. Do not use vocal signals to your horse when passing. The horse being passed may think they are meant for him.

10. One should pass another horse and rider to the inside of the ring. Those not passing should ride as close to the rail as possible.

11. When passing, leave a wide enough distance between horses to prevent kicking.

12. Do not cut another horse and rider off when passing. This is very rude to the other rider.

## TRAIL RULES

Once a student has some semblance of control of the horse and can post fairly rhythmically, he may begin to take short, slow trail rides. These trail rides are very important because they give the student a feel of the horse on terrain unlike that of the smooth, level ring. This is also a wonderful time to discover what a horse is really like when out of the familiar routine of ring work. The rider must exercise a little more control without a fence to guide the horse. The rider must learn to look ahead and be prepared for what is to come.

Proper procedure for trail riding.

The rider must also learn a new set of rules for his own safety as well as that of his horse and companions. Too many good riders are very discourteous because they have forgotten the fears of the novice, as well as his inability to control the horse while trying desperately to stay in the saddle. Too many riders are just plain inconsiderate of others and the result is a trail ride less than enjoyable.

1. The horse should be walked the first ten minutes to warm him up and give the rider a chance to get comfortable and relaxed. The horse should be walked the last ten minutes so that he is breathing normally and is fairly cooled out. The horse loves to return to the barn, his happy haven of comfort, and will often attempt to take advantage of the rider in his haste. Thus it is most important for the

rider to insist that his horse walk when within sight of the barn so that he learns that this is relaxing time and does not pull his rider's arms out of their sockets trying to run madly home. If the horse is extremely persistent in his attempts at speeding home, he should be turned around and walked away from the direction of home until he is walking in a relaxed manner, then turned again toward the barn. This little lesson should be continued until the horse gets the point.

2. Walk the horse on paved roads and up and down steep hills to eliminate the danger of his falling and to reduce the wear and tear on his legs. Walk the horse over bridges.

3. Do not let the horse eat leaves or grass on the trail or any other time when you are mounted. This can become a persistent and annoying habit.

4. Keep at least one horse's distance between horses for safety's sake.

5. Do not begin a faster gait without warning or consulting one's riding companion so he too may be prepared.

6. Never canter past a group of riders.

7. Do not move any faster than the poorest rider in the group can manage with ease.

8. When a strange vehicle approaches, try to move off the road; in any case, be prepared for the horse to shy.

9. Do not hold branches back. It is dangerous to the next rider to have to attempt to duck under a swinging branch which may otherwise swat him in the face.

10. When riding with a supervised group, always follow the lead horse and all directions given by the leader.

11. Warn others of approaching vehicles.

12. When crossing an intersection, or when crossing a busy road, the group should all cross at the same time. It is dangerous to have horses on both sides of the road when a car passes. The horses left behind usually try to get across the road to their friends and are oblivious to approaching traffic.

13. A group of riders should always ride on the same side of the road. It is difficult for the passing motorist to watch out for the horses on both sides of the road at the same time.

14. It is a good idea to face approaching traffic. The horse is better able to see the approaching vehicle, as is the rider. The car approaching from the rear will thus be far enough away from the horse as to eliminate maximum danger.

15. Halt the entire group of horses if one rider must stop for a

minute; otherwise his horse will not want to wait.

16. Be on the lookout for holes when riding in a strange field. Do not canter in a field unless the ground is very familiar, and then keep a lookout for new holes.

17. Do not ride in fields without the owner's permission, and do not ride in fields with growing crops. Nothing will make horses and riders more unwelcome.

18. Always be considerate of your horse and courteous to your companions.

19. The horse may be watered in a stream. If he is warm, he should be kept moving slowly after his drink. Be careful he does not try to lie down in the water to cool off!

20. If the horse is to be tied for a rest period, he should be tied by a neck rope or a halter slipped over his bridle. He should never be tied by his bridle alone as it is too easy to break. The girth of the saddle should be loosened or the saddle taken off completely.

Trail riding is a great deal of fun for both horse and rider if the rider just uses common sense. He must remember that the horse, unlike a bicycle or automobile, is unable to produce speed for a long period of time without becoming very tired. The considerate rider will alternate his gait and speed to suit the terrain and the condition of his horse. Certainly, maintaining one speed for a long time is not only boring but tiring. However, when the horse's breathing is becoming labored, he must be walked quietly until he is cool and relaxed. A trot is a relaxing, quieting gait also. A canter, especially in the exciting company of other horses, will tire a horse quickly. A horse seldom ridden will not be able to take much work at all; one that is consistently ridden every day or so can take quite a lot of work before showing signs of fatigue.

# 13.  Instruction

## THE RIDING INSTRUCTOR

Perhaps a chapter devoted to the riding instructor has no place in this book, a book for the beginning rider. However, it is hoped that such a book will find its place on the instructor's shelf as a reference or a book to be recommended to her students. A chapter of this sort may be welcome to the beginning instructor.

The riding instructor must first of all like children and people as well as horses. Many horse lovers and expert equestriennes have little patience with the beginning rider and thus must not consider themselves qualified to teach their favorite sport. Students must like and respect their instructor in order to learn the maximum taught. If they are afraid of or dislike their instructor, their lessons will not be continued for long.

The instructor must be able to intuit the horse's actions so that she knows what the horse plans to do, thus preventing accidents.

The instructor must remain calm in the face of an emergency, not only so as not to frighten the students, but also so as not to frighten the horses. She must be able to think and act quickly.

The instructor must have a good, clear speaking voice. She must be able to be heard over horses' hoof beats.

The instructor must be able to clearly explain each skill in a logical, progressive order. She must understand the parts which make up each skill so that she can understand why a student is having difficulty in a certain phase.

The instructor must know what she is doing at all times. When in doubt, she should not hesitate to consult a reference book or a

The start of a lesson. Note the lack of uniformity in beginners' positions, dress, etc.

more knowledgeable horseman. It certainly does no harm to admit that one is not certain of a particular point occasionally. The know-it-all continually demonstrates his ignorance.

Do not make statements that are not backed up with facts. A student will often ask how you know a certain fact, or why.is this true, and the instructor must be prepared with an answer.

The instructor should not threaten her students unless she is prepared to carry out the threat or she will lose their respect. Occasionally a student will get out of hand, especially in a camp situation where riding is required. The instructor may threaten to bring the student into the center of the ring until he decides to behave himself. If the student continues his annoying behavior, the instructor must carry out this threat or the student will become more of a behavior problem than ever.

The instructor must be able to decide when her students are ready, both physically and mentally, to go on to the next skill. If they are asked to do something they are incapable of, they will become very discouraged.

An instructor demonstrating correct leg position to a class.

The instructor should try to see that each student has some success before the lesson is over so he will be eager to return. For the same reason, the instructor should call the lesson to a halt with a fun game or at a point when the students are enjoying themselves the most. This motivation to return will also motivate the student to try his best.

Safety is the main factor for the instructor to consider at all times.

He must never ask the students to do anything which could cause an accident. An over-cautious instructor is appreciated by students and parents.

The instructor must know her students and horses well so that she may mount the students on horses they are easily capable of managing. It is very important for the beginning student to develop confidence in his horse. Once his confidence is developed, he will learn rapidly.

The instructor should correct each mistake his student makes as he sees it; however, a student must not be corrected on too many *different* things during one lesson. He is able to concentrate on only one or two things at a time, and too many corrections will only confuse and discourage him. If the entire class is having difficulty with a particular skill, it should be explained and demonstrated again.

The instructor should ask questions of the students to see how much they actually understand. Often their limited knowledge, or shyness, will not allow them to ask questions or even think of questions to ask.

The instructor should be imaginative enough to make the lessons interesting. This will keep the students' attention and make them eager for each lesson.

If the group is showing signs of restlessness, the instructor may begin some interesting exercises or games. Older students occasionally get leg cramps until their muscles are more used to riding. Occasionally a student may get a side ache. Anyone in pain should be allowed to bring his horse into the center of the ring to rest.

The class must be under control at all times for safety's sake as well as to provide the best learning situation. The instructor should follow a set procedure when instructing a class. A very workable procedure is outlined below:

1. Warm up for five minutes doing exercises and asking questions.
2. Review what has already been learned. Correct mistakes.
3. Introduce a new skill (if the class is ready) by:
   a. Explanation
   b. Demonstration—by instructor or assistant
   c. Practice
4. Rest period for horses and riders. The instructor may ask for parts of the horse, etc., or review the new skill.
5. Exercises at various gaits with and without stirrups and/or reins.

6. Practice new skill again. Too much practice of a new skill at one time becomes tiring because the student usually has so much difficulty at first. Shorter periods of practice are more beneficial and satisfying.

7. Cool out horses.

Beginners must be continuously drilled on all of the basic skills—mounting, dismounting, halting, circles, reverses, and, most important, the sitting trot. It is absolutely necessary for them to have a complete understanding of these, as they are the bases on which their later learning is structured. They must be taught to relax on the horse by means of exercises. The instructor must instill confidence in them and their ability to ride. Constant praise is welcome, as most students go through periods of discouragement when they feel they will never be able to ride well. All corrections can be made positively. For instance, a student may have trouble standing in the stirrups, a favorite basic exercise. The instructor should say, "Balance on your hands with your legs and feet directly underneath you" instead of "Don't stick your legs out in front of you." This negative attitude tells the student what he is doing wrong, but it does not help him in improving. The positive attitude tells the student in very plain terms how he is better able to improve the skill.

It is very helpful to have an assistant with a group of beginning riders if only to help them mount the horses and adjust the stirrups. This assistant can be a more advanced student eager to help and thus win the instructor's favor. It may be a student ambitious to teach equitation himself, and thus willing to help and observe the instructor. Assisting in the ring is an excellent opportunity for the student to see some of the mistakes he may be making. He will become more aware of how he can help himself in correcting them. One never learns so much as when one teaches or observes a teacher in action, because he discovers what he does not know and becomes more eager to learn.

## THE BEGINNING STUDENT

The beginning student, whether adult or child, has a particular reason for taking equitation lessons or he would not seek out an instructor. It helps the instructor plan his lessons if he fully understands the student's goal. As the student progresses, his goals may change as his understanding of horses and horsemanship increases. In any case, the instructor must realize that the beginner has had little

A beginning rider. Notice the left stirrup leather is incorrectly turned, toes are pointing out, etc.

contact with horses and respond accordingly. The unsympathetic instructor can just imagine how he would feel if presented with an elephant for the first time and told casually to "Mount up!" The beginning student, however brave he may seem, is generally scared to death. He is afraid to be too near the horse. He is afraid the horse will not like him. He is afraid of what the horse may do because he has no idea of what a horse *can* do. The beginner is afraid to discipline the horse. He is afraid the horse will react unfavorably. He is afraid of the other horses in the ring. He is afraid of speed or any movement which is unexpected. He is afraid that if he loses his stirrups he will fall off for certain.

The instructor will slowly build the student's confidence in the horse and in his own ability to control it. Relaxing exercises and continuous review of previous lessons are very necessary. The beginner is not only learning completely new and different skills which call for the use of a new set of muscles, he must also manage a very large animal at the same time. Working in the barn with the horse will help the student better understand the horse and his habits; this in turn builds love for and confidence in the horse. A relaxing trail ride later in his education will be welcome, as he will not have to be continually aware of his form.

Then there is the over-confident child who says he has ridden before—usually in a 25¢ around-the-ring pony ride—and expects to gallop away immediately. He is most chagrined when he discovers the instructor will not let him. My favorite motto—probably because I am a mother and have read innumerable books on the subject—is "One must learn to walk before he can learn to run." Then I follow with an explanation. This usually satisfies all but the most persistent youngster.

## EXERCISES

Below is a list of exercises which help a beginner accomplish various skills. Exercises, besides being very beneficial for muscle development and confidence, relieve the occasional monotony of the routine and drill that often make up a beginning class.

1. *Stand in the stirrups*—The student places his hands, with the reins, about halfway up the horse's neck. The hands are for balance only, so that the rider does not jerk on the reins when he loses his balance. The rider must not try to actively lean on the horse's neck; he is able to stand because of the strength in his legs and the balance of his weight. The rider's feet must be directly under his body; otherwise he will fall back down. The similarity between stirrups and the floor cannot be over-emphasized. Few people are able to maintain their balance when standing on the floor with their feet out in front of them. Few riders are able to stand in their stirrups with their feet and legs out in front of them. The purpose of this exercise is to develop balance, strengthen leg muscles, correctly position the legs and feet, and stretch out the leg muscles when warming up.

As the rider returns to the saddle he bends his knees only. The position his legs were in when he was standing should be maintained when he is sitting except that his knees are bent in a more acute

Standing in the stirrups.

angle. The student should do this exercise at a standstill at first, then at a walk and later at a trot. At a trot the student can feel his ankle joints absorb the shock of the gait. The student should be able to maintain the standing position several times around the ring after several lessons. This exercise may be turned into a game with the winner the last one to sit down. Later, when balance is more developed, the student tries this exercise without using his hands for balance. Care must be taken not to jerk the horse's mouth.

2. *Sit on paper or hold paper under the thigh or knee*—This is an exercise that can also be made into a game. The rider attempts to keep a piece of paper from falling to the ground at a sitting trot or canter. The last one to lose his paper is the winner. This exercise makes the student more aware of what parts of his body should not

Riding without stirrups.

leave the saddle, and helps him in educating his muscles accordingly.

3. *Riding without stirrups*—During the first lesson, the student should ride at a walk without stirrups for a short period of time. It is important that he not become too dependent on them for balance or else he may panic if he loses them. Later, when he is able to sit a trot in a relaxed manner, he should practice without stirrups. Care should be taken to see that he has a smooth gaited horse for the first few attempts. When the student posts fairly well he may begin posting without stirrups. This is very difficult at first, but once the rider can do it easily he will discover that his posting with stirrups is smoother, easier, and more natural. He learns to let the horse do the work.

Posting without stirrups. This rider is posting on the inside (incorrect) diagonal. Because she has lost her balance, the rider is attempting to regain it by over use of the reins.

It is important when riding without stirrups that the student maintain the leg position he would have if he were riding with stirrups. This is required when riding without stirrups in the show ring. It demonstrates greater leg control. It certainly does no harm to ask the student to ride with a relaxed leg without stirrups; the important thing is that both he and the instructor are aware of the importance of leg position also.

The student should attempt to pick up his stirrups without looking down. This will give him confidence in his ability to regain them should he lose them at an inopportune moment.

4. *Riding without reins*—This exercise is extremely important as it teaches the student not to depend on his hands and the horse's mouth for balance. It may be done on a lunge line with the student taking private lessons. For group instruction this exercise is done at a walk in a very organized fashion on quiet, cooperative horses. The student loops his arm through the reins and crosses his arms in front of his chest Indian fashion. The arms must be occupied in some

Riding without reins.

way or the student will continually attempt to regain his reins at first. It helps if the horses neck-rein because they are more easily guided with one hand and slack reins.

While the reins are held in this manner, the student may be asked to stand in the stirrups, bend down and touch the horse's neck with his forehead or any number of other bending and relaxing exercises. Later, a slow sitting trot or even a posting trot may be executed in this manner. Cantering without reins is better done with only one student in the ring for obvious reasons.

5. *Riding without reins and stirrups*—This is a wonderful exercise because the student learns to depend on his balance instead of the reins, stirrups, etc.

Clicking heels over horse's neck.

6. *Riding bareback*—An occasional bareback class is beneficial for balance and for allowing the student to feel the horse's back muscles at work. The students learn to love bareback riding once they adjust to the wiggly feeling of the horse's back.

7. *Various bending and relaxing exercises*—These include: 1) laying back on the horse's back with the feet still in the stirrups; 2) touching the heels over the horse's neck; 3) touching the heels over the horse's rump; 4) touching the toes with the fingers; 5) touching the tail with one hand, then the other; 6) touching the poll with one hand, then the other. Touching various parts of the horse helps the students learn where these parts are.

8. *Turning around in the saddle*—This is usually done at a stand-

Touching the toe with the fingers. Note the rider maintains the correct leg position.

Touching the dock of the horse's tail.

Reaching forward to touch between the horse's ears.

Bending down to touch the forehead to the horse's neck.

still but may be done at a walk with the more advanced students. The student turns a complete circle in his saddle. The first one to return to his original position is the winner.

Any number of exercises and games may be invented by the imaginative instructor. Old games may be adapted to playing on horseback. The children love them and their atitude toward ring riding and trying their very best is greatly improved when they enjoy what they are doing.

# 14. *Horsemanship Requirements*

Certain standards of achievement should be set up so that the student has more concrete evidence of his progress. These standards, when in chart form, will help initiate competition among the students. This competition in turn will cause the students to try a little harder; it gives them the boost they need. This is especially true when attempting to teach parts of the horse and so forth to the students who would rather just ride and forget the rest.

## REQUIREMENTS FOR THE BEGINNERS B
## HORSEMANSHIP AWARD

1. Mount correctly at all times.
2. Measure and adjust the stirrups correctly from the ground before mounting.
3. Dismount correctly at all times.
4. Circle and reverse correctly.
5. Be able to halt a horse correctly from a walk and trot.
6. Be able to ask a horse to walk correctly from a halt upon command.
7. Be able to ask a horse to trot correctly from a walk or halt upon command.
8. At a walk, be able to drop stirrups, maintain correct position, and pick up the stirrups without looking down.
9. Be able to maintain good position of hands, legs, and seat at a walk.
10. Be able to sit a slow trot well.
11. Be able to post in fair form.

12. Know the five main colors of the horse.
13. Know all the ring rules and practice them.
14. Know the markings of the horse.
15. Be able to execute beginners' exercises easily:
    a. Stand in the stirrups at a walk with or without use of hands for balance.
    b. Ride without reins at a walk.
    c. Ride without reins and stirrups at a walk.
    d. Various other bending and relaxing exercises.
16. Know and practice all the stable rules.

## REQUIREMENTS FOR THE BEGINNER A HORSEMANSHIP AWARD

1. Be able to lead the horse in and out of the stall when asked; this includes fastening him correctly if necessary.

2. Be able to stop, start, and turn the horse correctly at a walk with and without stirrups.

3. Circle and reverse correctly at a sitting trot with and without stirrups.

4. Be able to maintain a steady trot at all times.

5. Be able to ride a posting and sitting trot in good form.

6. Know the reasons for posting on the correct diagonal; use the correct diagonal consistently.

7. Be able to unsaddle and unbridle the horse correctly. This includes wiping or soaping the tack, hanging it up correctly, etc.

8. Be able to execute a Figure 8 at a walk, sitting trot, and posting trot correctly. This includes changing diagonals.

9. Be able to tighten the girth and adjust the stirrups from the saddle.

10. Have fair control of self and horse when working with a group in the ring.

11. Know what to do in case of emergencies.

12. Execute brief canter without regard to leads.

13. Execute flying dismount from a halt and walk.

14. Understand the correct use of each grooming tool; be able to groom a horse completely and correctly.

15. Know trail rules and practice them when on a trail ride.

16. Be able to trot without stirrups; be able to pick up stirrups at a trot without looking down.

17. Become proficient in the following exercises:
    a. Stand in the stirrups at a trot.
    b. Ride without reins at a sitting and posting trot.
    c. Ride without reins and stirrups at a sitting trot.
    d. Various other exercises.
18. Be able to execute turns, halts, circles, etc. at a definite place when walking or doing a sitting trot.

## REQUIREMENTS FOR THE INTERMEDIATE B HORSEMANSHIP AWARD

1. Have good control of self and horse when in the ring.
2. Be able to execute a serpentine at a trot with a correct change of diagonals.
3. Accomplish reasonably accurate transitions from walk to trot to walk to halt.
4. Maintain an even speed at a trot while executing circles and reverses.
5. Execute a flying dismount from a trotting horse.
6. Be able to post without stirrups and regain them without looking.
7. Know all the parts of the saddle, bridle, and horse.
8. Know the meaning of the term, "aids." Know the natural and artificial aids.
9. Know the reasons for cantering on the inside lead in the ring.
10. Have very good balance and seat at a walk and trot, and good balance at a canter.
11. Be able to tie a horse correctly with a bowline knot.
12. Be able to correctly saddle and bridle a horse.
13. Know the various types of equipment used on a horse and why.
14. Ride bareback at a walk and trot.
15. Be able to ride a horse correctly on contact.

## REQUIREMENTS FOR THE INTERMEDIATE A HORSEMANSHIP AWARD

1. Be able to put the horse on the correct canter lead consistently; know what lead he is on. Be able to maintain a canter until asked to halt. Canter departure should be smooth.

2. Canter without stirrups.

3. Be able to back the horse correctly.

4. Be able to reverse and circle at a canter.

5. Be able to execute two speeds at the walk, three at the trot, and two at the canter.

6. Understand collection and be able to execute a collected walk, trot, and canter fairly well.

7. Understand stable management; be able to pass the written test.

8. Know the main breeds of horses, their origin, usage, basic characteristics, distinctions, etc.

9. Understand how to clean tack.

10. Be alert to any abnormalities in tack or horse.

11. Ride bareback at a walk, trot, and canter in fair form.

12. Understand what is meant by "extended" gaits and be able to execute them.

13. Know the parts of the hoof and their functions.

## REQUIREMENTS FOR THE ADVANCED B HORSEMANSHIP AWARD

1. Ride the balanced seat in excellent form with the correct use of aids.

2. Be able to ride bareback at all three gaits with good control and balance.

3. Maintain a canter in a group canter around the ring.

4. Have excellent control of both self and horse in the ring and on the trail.

5. Execute the three speeds of the canter.

6. Practice canter departures on a designated lead.

7. Be able to execute a Figure 8 at a canter, changing leads in the center.

8. Know the characteristics and faults of a good pleasure horse.

9. Know common unsoundnesses and blemishes.

10. Be able to fit a saddle and bridle to the horse.

11. Understand the function of horseshoes and shoeing.

12. Be able to ride all three gaits with a Weymouth bridle. Understand its function.

13. Be able to bandage a horse's legs for shipping.

14. Have some experience driving a horse in a cart; this includes harnessing.

## REQUIREMENTS FOR THE ADVANCED A HORSEMANSHIP AWARD

1. Be able to execute a serpentine at a canter with the correct change of leads.

2. Be able to execute a Figure 8 at a canter with a flying change of leads.

3. Be able to execute a canter with a change of leads every six strides.

4. Be able to estimate a horse's age by his teeth.

5. Be able to work a horse on a lunge line.

6. Understand basic principles of horse training; have the opportunity to work with a young horse.

7. Begin elementary dressage.

8. Be able to lead a horse into a trailer; understand trailering procedure.

9. Begin jumping exercises; low jumps over a course.

10. Know first aid to horse and rider in case of emergencies.

These requirements for awards have been realistically designed from experience. Unfortunately, not too many students continue instruction into an advanced stage unless they plan to show in Equitation classes at horse shows. Too many of them buy a pleasure horse, and upon acquiring the horse, discontinue lessons. It would seem logical to continue lessons for this very reason, but most people are satisfied with pleasure riding for the fun of it as opposed to the detailed study of equitation.

This is the reason that many skills listed in the award requirements are skimmed over or not mentioned in this text; this book was designed to be a simple explanation—details have been eliminated. The instructor, not this book, should be the source of detail.

# 15. *Your First Horse*

The decision to buy a horse is not lightly made by most horse lovers. There are many points to be carefully thought out. Probably the most important is whether one actually can afford to maintain a horse and whether he actually wants to. Boarding rates vary with location. They may be as high as $75.00 a month in a metropolitan area and as low as $25.00 a month in a very rural area. If one has his own stable the expense will be less because he is not paying for extra labor. Of course, if one puts his horse in training, too, the cost may be up to $150.00 a month.

One may also consider the responsibility of owning a horse. Unless one is caring for his own animal, his responsibility will be at a minimum. The stable boarding the horse is responsible for his feed and stall care. Usually a large stable also maintains responsibility for worming the horse and keeping him correctly shod. Having the horse groomed and exercised will add a little to the basic boarding fee, but if the stable owner will turn the horse out into a paddock several times a week, this should cost nothing extra. The owner's main responsibility will be his care of the horse when he is riding him. Unless a groom is available to cool the horse out, it is the owner's job to be sure the horse is cooled out properly before he leaves for home. He must also be considerate of the horse during the ride.

Another point to consider is just exactly what type of horse one wants. If one is taking lessons or has taken lessons, he should consult his instructor who will be glad to give his opinion on the subject. Perhaps he may be able to help locate a suitable horse. For the first horse, if it is to be a pleasure horse as opposed to a show horse, the buyer should not be particularly opinionated as to color, age, or breed. His goal should be to locate a well trained, smooth gaited, mature horse, preferably at least 8 years old, that will help him better understand the species. Many people buy a young, spirited, beautiful horse for themselves or their children only to discover that the horse becomes unmanageable. The horse is sold at a loss to the first person brave enough to trailer him away. A good horse has been spoiled and a family that may have developed a very active interest in the horse world soon turns to raising tropical fish or something equally as safe. The horse is blamed, but it is the owner who is at fault; a horse responds to the wishes of his owner, but if one does not know how to communicate or enforce his wishes, the horse will become confused and go his own way. An older horse is more settled in his ways and his training is firmly fixed in his mind. He is not easily frightened or startled by things a novice can do to him. His mouth may be somewhat calloused so is not as sensitive to pain as that of a young horse. Physically and mentally he is able to survive until the novice has gained more experience; if he is patient enough, he is even able to help the novice gain that experience.

A horse may be purchased from a dealer, breeding farm, or private owner. A novice should avoid auctions unless he knows the horse being auctioned. An auction is a marvelous place to see an assortment of horses and their problems; a wealth of knowledge may be gained there, but too often the horse purchased on the spur of the moment is a white elephant useful to no one.

Some of the things to look for in a first horse include a well shaped head with large, bright eyes. This usually denotes a kind disposition, a very important factor. The horse's head and general facial expression can tell one quite a bit about his personality. He should be interested in people, sniffing and curious. His ears should never go back when one approaches. This denotes a sour disposition, a horse that is tired and bored with humanity. A gelding usually has more personality than a mare. A stallion should never be considered.

The horse must have sound legs. This means no swelling or enlarged tendons. His joints must be clearly outlined as opposed to being filled with fluid. A splint will not harm the horse and will seldom cause lameness. Scarred knees could indicate a horse that stumbles and falls frequently. Scarred ankles or pasterns could indicate a horse that hits himself with his hind feet. A veterinarian should be consulted and should advise on the final purchase of a horse.

## PARTS OF THE HORSE

A. Ears.
B. Poll (Bone between horse's ears).
C. Forelock or foretop.
D. Forehead.
E. Face.
F. Nostril.
G. Upper lip.
H. Lower lip.
I. Chin.
J. Cheek.
K. Muzzle.
L. Throat latch.
M. Throat.
N. Neck.
O. Crest (Arch on top of neck).
P. Mane.
Q. Barrel.
R. Shoulder.
S. Point of Shoulder (joint).
T. Chest.
U. Brisket (Between front legs).
V. Forearm.
W. Elbow.
X. Knee.
Y. Cannon bone.
Z. Fetlock joint.
1. Pastern.
2. Hock joint.
3. Chestnut (small boney growth on all four legs; a left-over toe from the Dawn Age).
4. Tail.
5. Thigh.
6. Point of buttock.
7. Point of hip.
8. Flank.
9. Stifle (joint comparable to the human knee cap).
10. Gaskin (muscle).
11. Stomach.
12. Dock of tail (bone-extension of the spine).
13. Rump or croup.
14. Withers.
15. Back.
16. Loin.
17. Hip.
18. Coronary band or coronet (where hoof joins leg).
19. Hoof.
20. Ergot (Small boney growth; a left-over toe from the Dawn Age).

The horse should be short in the back. He will be easier to keep fat. His ribs should look like a barrel casing, round and smooth. This provides ample room for his vital organs. His rump should be round and flat and his withers not too prominent. Boney withers are subject to saddle sores if the saddle does not fit just right. The horse's shoulder angle should be at least 45 degrees. A straighter angle is usually associated with straight pasterns, which not only create uncomfortable gaits, but also predispose the horse to such lamenesses as ringbone, sidebone, and navicular.

The horse should not be heavey, a condition similar to asthma in humans. Even though it does not seem serious at the moment, it is incurable and becomes increasingly worse, especially if the horse must be stabled in a dusty barn or in the late summer when it is dry and hot.

One should never consider a blind or deaf horse for obvious reasons. A very thin horse should be looked upon with skepticism, too, because his whole disposition may alter when he is fat again. He may become too spirited for the novice when his concern for food diminishes and his strength returns to normal.

The horse should appear calm and willing when mounted by a beginner. He should not toss his head and fret because he resents a bit. He should not shy away when being saddled. He should be willing to travel in the company of strange horses without becoming aggressive toward them or nervous when he is at the end of the group. He should be accustomed to traffic sights and sounds.

After the selection of the horse and the okay of a knowledgeable horseman, preferably a veterinarian, the prospective buyer should try to make arrangements for a week's trial period before actually purchasing the horse. This trial period is a good chance to really spend time with the horse—grooming him, riding him, and so forth—to discover if indeed this is the horse of your choice.

After purchasing the horse the new owner should make every effort to continue his education in horse care and equitation so he will not thoughtlessly abuse his animal because of a lack of knowledge. The horse is at the mercy of his owner, and the owner should be willing to assume the responsibility of seeing that the horse is given the best.

# Glossary

This list of defined terms is by no means complete; it is merely a glossary of terms used in this book which may otherwise confuse the novice.

ACTIVE HAND: The opening and closing of the rider's fingers in rhythm with the horse's stride. The active hand prevents the horse from bracing his poll (part between the horse's ears) and neck against the rider's puny strength when turning or halting. An active hand constantly reminds the horse of the command.

AIDS: Aids are the means by which the rider talks to his horse. These are natural aids—hands, legs, feet, weight, voice; artificial aids—whip, spurs, martingale; and mental aids—the rider makes up his mind as to what he intends the horse to do and the horse uses his mind to translate the signal into action. He does this from his memory of what has been taught to him. These aids must be coordinated so that the horse is able to translate them effectively. The rider's use of the aids must coordinate the forehand and hindquarters of the horse's body; the legs are not used without the support of the hands and the hands are not used without the support of the legs.

AMATEUR: One who rides or shows horses for love, not money.

ANIMATION: Lively, vigorous way of moving.

ATTIRE: Manner of dress.

BARS OF THE MOUTH: The space in the horse's lower jaw between the incisors and molars. The bit acts upon this sensitive area.

BENDING THE HORSE: The act of causing the horse's body to form an arc by the correct use of the aids. In a turn, the horse's hind feet should follow the path made by the front feet if the body is correctly bent or curved.

BIGHT OF THE REINS: The leftover end of the reins which falls over the horse's right shoulder.

BILLET STRAPS: The straps under the flap of the saddle. The girth is attached to them to hold the saddle in place.

BIT: The metal bar in the horse's mouth by which the rider communicates with and controls the horse.

"BLOW OUT": The act of taking a deep breath in order to expand his chest when the horse is being saddled. This is a defense so that the one saddling him is unable to get the girth tight.

BOWLINE KNOT: A knot useful for tying a horse because it is quick and easy to untie in an emergency. If the horse pulls back against the rope, it is impossible for this knot to tighten to the point of being virtually impossible to untie.

BOX STALL: A large stall usually about 12 feet by 12 feet in size. The horse is loose in this type of stall.

BREAK A GAIT: When a horse changes from one gait to another. For example, a horse breaks from a canter to a trot.

BRIDLE: The leather headpiece which hold the bit in the horse's mouth when being ridden.

BRIDLEWISE: A horse that has been taught to neckrein is considered bridlewise.

CANTLE: The back of the saddle seat.

CAVESSON: A headstall which is attached to the bridle, coming down and around the horse's muzzle. It keeps the horse's mouth closed. It prevents his shifting the bit around in his mouth. It is necessary if the horse wears a standing martingale.

CHANGE OF HANDS: To change directions, as during a Figure 8 or reverse.

COLIC: A condition which can cause death due to failure of the heart from gas pressure or because of a twisted intestine due to the horse's thrashing around in pain. It is caused by feeding poor quality feed, over-feeding, poisonous weeds, feeding grain or too much water when the horse is over-heated or over-tired. Symptoms are restlessness, sweating, biting the flanks, lying down and getting up repeatedly, and other signs of pain and distress. The veterinarian should be called at once and the horse walked until he arrives.

COLLECTION: A horse in a state of collection takes shorter, more elevated strides. His neck is raised and arched. His hindquarters are well under him. A collected horse is alert and prepared to do his rider's bidding upon the slightest command.

COLLECTING THE HORSE: Collection is obtained by a stronger than normal use of legs to drive the horse forward into the hands, which will restrain him to a greater degree than normal. The forward impulse is restrained; the horse's energy is then directed into a very animated way of going as opposed to the speed which would result if the hands were not used correctly. A horse cannot maintain collection for long periods, as it is tiring; however, he should be trained to go in a collected manner when asked.

COLLECTING THE REINS: The act of gathering the reins; the act of shortening the reins in preparation for a signal.

COLORS: See Appendix A.

COLT: A young horse to about three years of age; usually refers to the young male.

CONDITIONING THE HORSE: Making a horse physically fit for whatever type of work he is expected to do.

CONFORMATION: The build of a horse.

A collected canter, left lead.

Cooler.

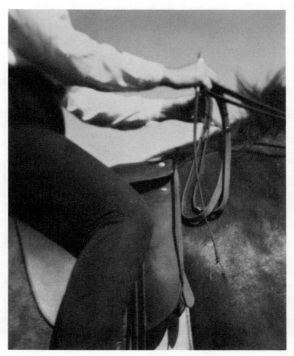

The correct way to hold a crop or whip. It is held in the palm of the hand with the reins. The beginner should use it on the horse's shoulder. It should be held to the inside of the ring during instruction, but in the right hand in the show ring.

COOLER: A wool blanket which covers the horse from head to tail. It is worn by a hot horse until he is cooled out or by a horse after being sponged off. It prevents the horse's cooling too fast and becoming chilled.

CRIBBING STRAP: A leather strap worn tightly around the throat of a horse that sucks air (a nervous habit called cribbing). This prevents his sucking air by not allowing him to expand his windpipe.

CROP: A long leather covered stick of wood, steel, or plastic with a leather wrist loop at one end and a folded leather thong at the other end. This is used for signalling and disciplining the horse.

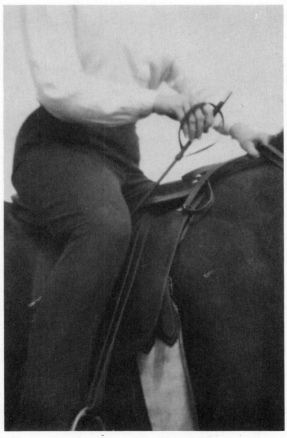

The rider places the crop or whip between thigh and saddle so her hands are free to tighten the girth or perform any other activity with which the crop might interfere. A crop should never be carelessly handled.

A horse in cross ties.

CROSS TIE: A horse should be tied for safety when groomed or otherwise handled. Cross-tying is a method of tying the horse when working with him. A rope or chain is fastened to the two opposite walls in the aisle of the barn or in the horse's stall. There is a snap on the dangling ends of each rope or chain. These snap on each side of the noseband of the horse's halter. There should be a minimum of slack. Because the horse's head is so confined, he is limited in his amount of movement.

CURB BIT: A bit with a straight or port mouthpiece with a shank at each end of the mouthpiece. It has a lever action when used in conjunction with a curb chain or chin strap (leather strap which takes the place of a curb chain). It is never used without a curb chain or strap. This action causes the horse to tuck in his chin as he flexes at the poll. The longer the shanks and the higher the port, the more severe is the bit. It should not be used on a colt until he has readily accepted the snaffle bit. Western horses are usually ridden on a curb bit alone, but they are also ridden on a loose rein. An English horse is ridden more on contact, so a curb bit alone can be very painful and distressing to the horse when used in this manner, especially by a rider with heavy or unsteady hands.

CURB CHAIN: A series of steel links that hook to the curb bit by curb hooks. This keeps the bit in the correct position in the horse's mouth as well as working with the bit to produce a lever action when the reins are pulled. The pressure on the lower jaw and behind the horse's ears pulls the jaw and chin toward the body, causing the horse

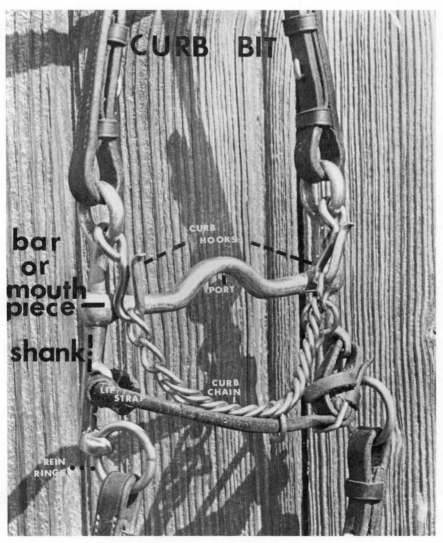

Curb bit with curb chain and lip strap.

to bend at the poll and arch his neck. It also aids in collecting the horse, as it causes him to get his hind legs under him and pull himself together. A leather curb or chin strap may be substituted.

DISMOUNT: The act of getting off the horse.

DOCK: The horse's tail bone; an extension of his spine.

DRESSAGE: A form of equitation in which the horse is taught advanced schooling movements. This aids in suppling the horse, making him more a pleasure to ride and more obedient to the aids. It is often called "High School" riding or Haute Ecole. The literal meaning is "training." It is not to be confused with the so-called dressage of the circus horses.

EQUINE: Refers to a horse.

EQUESTRIAN: One who rides horseback.

EQUITATION: The art of horseback riding.

EQUITATION CLASSES: Horse show classes in which the rider only is judged, as opposed to other classes in which the horse is judged.

An extended canter. Note the length of the horse as compared to the length of the horse in the illustration of the collected canter.

EXTENDED GAITS: As opposed to collected gaits, the extended gaits are executed with a lowered head and stretched neck. The horse appears relaxed and moves his legs easily with a long, low stride. These can be executed over long periods.

FEEL: Through his seat and hands the rider feels the muscular tensions of the horse; he feels what the horse is about to do as well as what he is doing. The rider must be relaxed in order to receive the massage from the horse. By feeling, the rider is able to understand the horse's movements and correct any false action.

FEELING THE HORSE'S MOUTH: The rider's contact with the horse's mouth through the reins and bit. The rider uses his ability to feel for purposes of control.

FLEXING: Refers to bending.

FOLLOWING HAND: The hand should follow the movements of the horse's head. The hands should always maintain a light contact with the horse's mouth.

FOUNDER (laminitis) : A disease of the foot affecting the blood vessels and sensitive tissue under the wall of the hoof. This is very painful and many times incurable, as the tissue is permanently injured. The tissue swells and, as it cannot expand due to the hard covering of the wall of the hoof, the pain is excessive. Horses suffering from a bad case of founder will groan and sweat and refuse to stand. The hoof becomes distorted in its growth. It is caused by bad quality feed, too much heatening food when the horse is not getting enough exercise, overwork, too fast work before being properly warmed up, or allowing the horse to stand (particularly in a draft) when he is hot. Symptoms are great heat in the walls of the hoof and excessive lameness. He walks as if he were on eggs. A foundered horse should stand in cold running water. His shoes should be removed. The veterinarian should be called.

GAIT: The horse's way of going. Most horses are born with three natural gaits—the walk, trot, and canter. There are other gaits such as a pace and running walk that are natural to some horses. There are also some artificial gaits such as the rack which man teaches to the horse.

GELDING: A mature male horse that has been castrated. A gelding is more docile than a stallion.

GIRTH: The "belt" that goes under the horse's stomach to hold the saddle in place.

GRASS BELLY: Sometimes called hay belly. A large stomach resembling that of a mare in foal; caused by too much grass or hay and not enough exercise.

GRAZE: Feed on growing grass or pasture.

GREEN HORSE: A horse with a minimum of training; the definition of this term varies with whomever is using it and for what reason.

HACK: To hack (verb) refers to pleasure riding. A hack (noun) refers to a pleasure horse.

HACKAMORE: A bitless bridle. The action is on the horse's nose, cutting off his wind. Hackamores are generally used on Western horses; however, they are very good for horses with very hard mouths or very soft mouths.

HALF-TURN: To reverse direction.

HALTER: The piece of leather equipment the horse wears on his head when being led, tied in a stall, or when in pasture. It is similar to a bridle but without the reins and bit.

HAND: Unit used in measuring the horse. There are four inches to a hand.

HANDS: Good hands, as an aid, are one of the most difficult accomplishments. The rider must acquire a sensitivity to his horse as well as excellent balance so as to use his hands independently. They must not follow his body movements. The rider must know the correct method of using the reins, along with the other aids, and do so with skill and tact so as to obtain the best possible response from each horse without causing him unnecessary discomfort. The rider must not use his hands for balance or to maintain position. The hands must be steady, they must be light enough to maintain just the merest contact with the horse's mouth. They must be firm and demand obedience when necessary. They must give the horse confidence and support.

HEAVY HANDS: A rider is considered heavy handed when he must use his horse's mouth for balance. The horse constantly shows signs of distress such as his tossing head, sour expression, and nervous manner. The heavy handed rider over-emphasizes all signals. The reins are always tight, for such a rider is usually afraid and displays his fear through the reins.

HORSE: Any equine over fourteen hands, two inches (58 inches) is considered a horse. Some of the horse breeds originating in the United States are the Standardbred (harness race horse), American Saddlebred, Quarter Horse, Morgan, and Tennessee Walking Horse.

HUNTER: A horse used on a mounted fox hunt.

INSIDE OF THE RING: The part of the ring closest to the center.

INTERFERING: The horse strikes his front foot with his hind foot when traveling. Horses that are tired or over-extended may interfere.

JUMPER: A horse trained to jump competitively; not as quiet and well-mannered as a hunter. A jumper is required to jump higher than a hunter.

LEAD SHANK: A leather strap with about an 18 inch chain which snaps to the horse's halter. It is used for leading the horse. The chain may be put over the horse's nose or under his chin for greater control in the case of a difficult horse.

LIP STRAP: A narrow leather strap (sometimes a chain) running through the ring in the curb chain and fastened to both shanks of the curb bit. It helps keep the curb chain in proper position. It prevents the loss of the curb chain should it come loose from both curb hooks. It prevents the horse's grabbing the shanks of the bit in his mouth.

MARE: A mature female horse.

MARTINGALE: There are two types of martingales, both with their separate functions. The running martingale (see illustration) prevents the horse from raising his head high enough to avoid the correct use of the snaffle bit on the bars of the mouth. Should the horse raise his head up, the reins continue to provide the correct action of the bit.

The standing martingale is attached to the cavesson and is used on "star gazers"—horses that continually carry their head and noses high. Any horse that needs a standing martingale needs a reschooled mouth more.

NEAR SIDE OF THE HORSE: The horse's left side.

NOVICE: A horse or rider is a novice until he has won three first place ribbons in his division at horse shows. Novice also refers to a rider of little experience.

OFF SIDE OF THE HORSE: The horse's right side.

OUTSIDE OF THE RING: The part of the ring closest to the fence.

PARASITE: An animal or plant that lives on, with, or in another animal or plant from which it gets its food.

PASTURE: Fenced grassland for livestock.

PELHAM BRIDLE: This type of bridle has a single curb bit to which are attached two sets of reins. The top rein is called the snaffle rein, as it produces an effect similar to that of a snaffle bit. The

A pelham bridle—one bit with two sets of reins.

lower rein is called the curb rein, as its action is like that of a curb bit. The bit has a curb chain or strap that is brought into play only when the curb bit is used. This type of bridle is used mostly with hunters, jumpers, and pleasure horses. (See "Weymouth bridle" for information on how to hold two pairs of reins correctly)

POMMEL: The front part of the saddle.

PONY: Usually any equine fourteen hands, two inches (58 inches) and under is considered a pony even though both his parents may be horses. Ponies are hardier than horses, and possibly more intelligent and wily because of their less pampered beginnings. They make good pets and mounts for children because of their small size, but they do have a tendency to be more independent thinkers than horses and take advantage of as much freedom as their young masters will allow them.

POSTING: The act of the rider's rising and sitting in rhythm with the two beat trot. Posting originated with the old time postmen who rode for hours delivering the mail. They discovered it was less tiring to both horse and rider to rise and sit when the horse was trotting. This movement thus became known as "posting."

PROFESSIONAL: Any horseman who earns money in the horse field, whether teaching, training, boarding, buying, or selling.

QUARTER HORSE: See illustration.

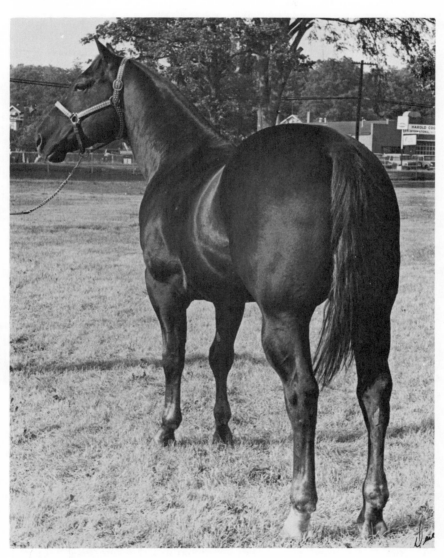

The Quarter Horse, a powerfully built, stocky horse developed in Virginia for ¼ mile racing, is now used mostly for ranch work, pleasure riding and showing.

RESET SHOES: The horse's shoes are pulled, his feet trimmed, and the shoes nailed back on. This is done when the shoes are not worn.

RING BONE: A boney enlargement above the coronary band caused by too much concussion from overwork on hard ground. The cartilage becomes ossified due to calcium deposits. The tendency toward this condition is considered hereditary.

SADDLE PAD OR BLANKET: A pad or blanket used under the saddle for protection to both saddle and horse. This should always be used except in the show ring. It should be made of a highly absorbent material such as felt or sheepskin.

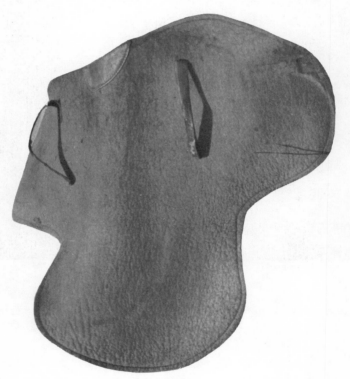

Felt saddle pad.

SAFETY CATCH: The metal catch which holds the stirrup leather to the saddle. If the rider is in danger of hanging by one foot from the saddle, this catch releases the stirrup leather and frees the rider.

SEAT: The seat refers to the style of riding—forward seat, saddle seat, balanced seat. It may refer to the general appearance of the rider on the horse—"He has a good seat."

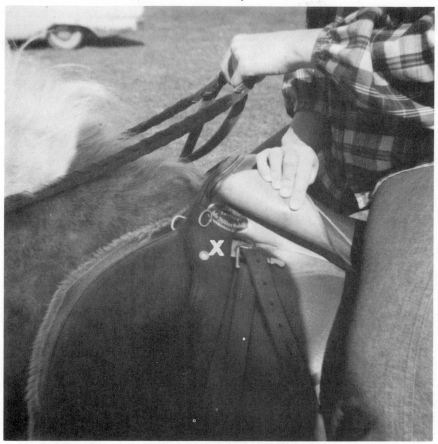

The safety catch.

SIDE BONE: Similar to ring bone except the enlargement is located at the side of the pastern.

SIRE: Father of a horse.

SNAFFLE BIT: A bit with a jointed mouthpiece. It has a nutcracker action on the horse's mouth. It works on the horse's lips as well as on the bars of the mouth. It tends to cause the horse to raise his head. Colts should begin their training bitted with a snaffle because they will better learn to accept this mild bit and will thus develop a good mouth. The thicker the mouthpiece, the milder is the action. Hunters, jumpers, and pleasure horses are generally ridden on a snaffle.

SQUARE TROT: When executing a square trot, the diagonal pair of legs hit the ground at exactly the same time. The rhythm is even

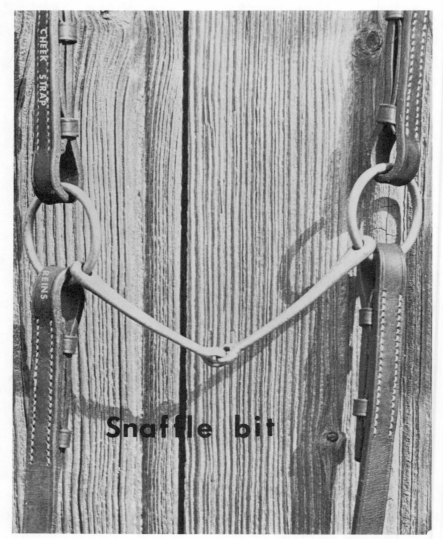

Snaffle bit. This snaffle is a thin one used with a curb bit in a Weymouth bridle. A snaffle used alone should have a thicker mouthpiece.

and defined as opposed to the horse that may hesitate a bit before striking the ground with one leg of the diagonal pair. This is hardly noticeable to the novice because the legs *seem* to strike the ground at the same time. The square trot is very easy to post to; the other is not.

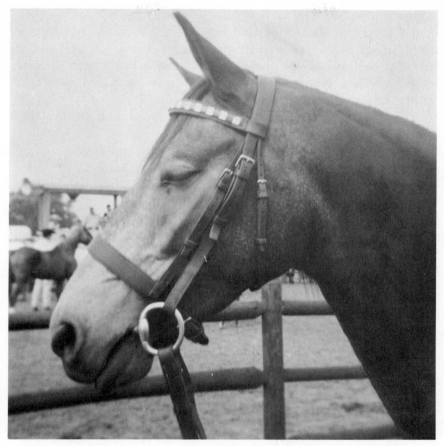

Snaffle bridle.

STABLE BLANKET: A blanket that covers the horse from his withers to his tail. It is fastened at the horse's chest and by two surcingles which go under his stomach and fasten on the left side of the blanket. A heavy blanket is used in the winter for warmth and to keep the horse's coat finer and easier to care for. A light blanket (sheet) is used in the summer to keep a show horse's coat in the best condition. A horse that has been clipped must wear a blanket so that he will not become chilled.

STALLION: A mature male horse.

STANDING STALL (tie stall): A stall about 7 feet by 5 feet in which the horse is tied at all times with a halter and rope. It has an open end at the back by which the horse enters and leaves.

STRETCH (park): The pose of a show horse when lined up for the judge's inspection. The horse's front legs are together and perpendicular to the ground. His hind legs are together but out behind him. This gives the appearance of a straighter top line and underline. It hides crooked hind legs and disguises a bad rump. Western horses, Arabians, hunters, and jumpers are not required to stretch.

STRIDE: The length of the horse's step.

SWEAT SCRAPER: An aluminum or wooden tool similar to the letter J, with curved edges. This is used to scrape excess water or sweat from the horse in an attempt to hasten the drying process.

TACK: Short for tackle. Refers to the equipment used on the horse (noun). To tack (verb) the horse refers to saddling and bridling him. To untack refers to unsaddling and unbridling.

TRANSITION: To change from one condition to another; changing from one gait to another.

A horse standing in a stretch.

Two methods of holding the reins of a weymouth or pelham bridle. The difference is whether the rider prefers to divide the reins with one or two fingers.

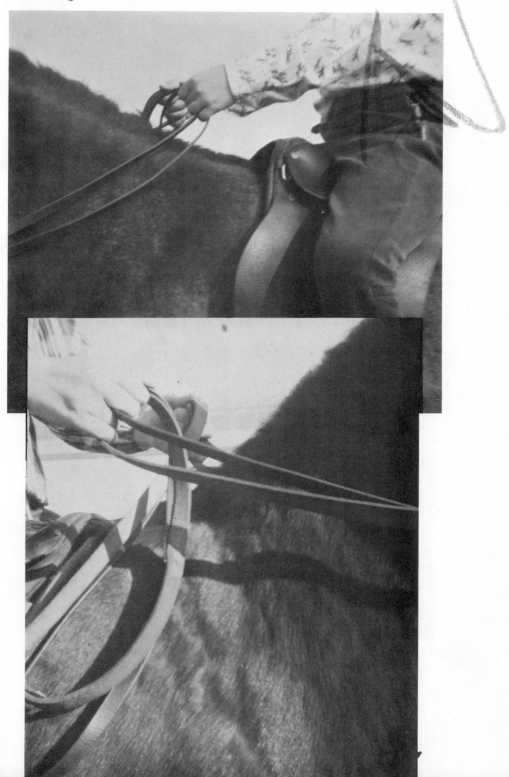

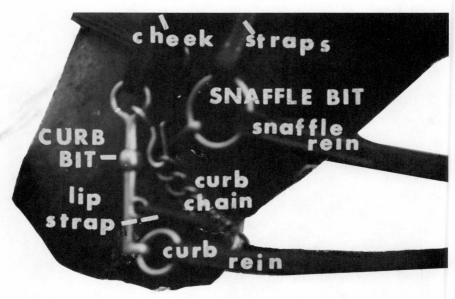

A Weymouth bit set.

WEYMOUTH BRIDLE: Also known as a full bridle or double bridle. A weymouth bridle consists of two bits, a snaffle and a curb, with a cheek strap and rein attached to each. This type of bridle is used mainly on dressage horses and show horses because the action of the two bits aids the rider in obtaining good collection, balance, and head carriage. The horse is guided and controlled on the snaffle, while the curb maintains collection and head carriage.

Because the snaffle rein is used most, it is held under the little finger as when riding with a single rein bridle. The curb rein is held either between the ring finger and little finger or between the ring finger and middle finger. The latter is preferred because the rider is more aware of the location of this rein and is able to use it better because he has more flexibility and strength in the middle finger. The curb rein goes between the snaffle rein and the horse's neck; it is the inside rein.

The snaffle rein should be thicker than the curb reins and should be buckled at the bight instead of sewn (as are the curb reins) so that a running martingale may be easily attached if necessary.

WHIP: Similar to a crop except longer, more flexible, and having a lash end. The whip is more severe than a crop and should not be used by a beginner.

# *Appendix A*

## COLORS OF THE HORSE

Horses come in many different colors and patterns of color. A sure sign of a novice is ignorance of the correct terms for these various colors. Color makes no difference to the usefulness of a horse, but some people do prefer one color to another.

1. BLACK: The coat is black, although sometimes it turns reddish-brown from the sun.

2. BAY: Bays come in shades from tan to dark brown and *always* have a black mane, tail, forelock, and four black stockings (called points). A sandy bay horse is light brown; a blood bay is a reddish, medium brown, and a mahogany bay is a dark, rich brown.

3. SEAL BROWN: A seal brown horse has a coat so dark brown that it looks black. The distinguishing features are light tan markings around the eyes, muzzle, flanks, insides of the thighs, and on the stomach. Mules are often this color.

4. CHESTNUT: Chestnuts come in shades from yellow-gold to a very dark reddish-brown. The mane and tail are usually the same color as the body, although they may be several shades lighter. Some even have a flaxen (creamy white) mane and tail. A liver chestnut is a dark auburn color similar to the color of liver. A red chestnut, often called a sorrel, is a definite red color.

5. GRAY: A gray horse has a mixture of white and black hairs. A gray horse is usually born almost black, becoming increasingly whiter as he grows older. A gray horse always has black skin. The mane and tail may be black, white, or gray. The black and white hairs generally form various patterns. A dapple gray horse seems

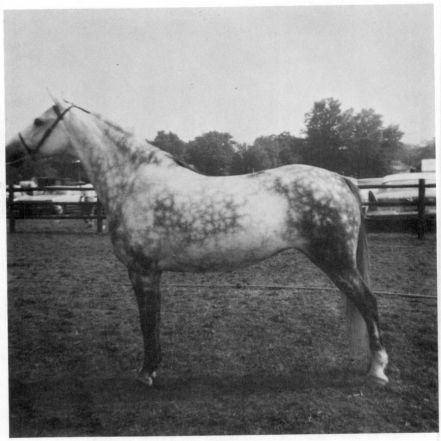

A dapple gray Welsh mare pony.

to have a pattern of little circles on his body. A flea-bitten gray horse has small, colored spots that resemble large fleas from a distance. An iron or steel gray horse has more black hairs than white. This usually indicates a young horse.

6. ROAN: A roan horse has an even mixture of white hairs with hairs of any other color. A blue roan has an even mixture of black and white hairs; a strawberry roan has an even mixture of chestnut and white hairs, and a bay roan has an even mixture of brown and white hairs with a black mane and tail and stockings.

7. DUN: A dun horse is usually a yellowish color and always has a dorsal stripe, a stripe running the length of the spine. The most common dun color is buckskin. A buckskin is yellow with a black

Appaloosa.

mane and tail and stockings, and a black dorsal stripe. Dun usually denotes a washed out color.

8. PALOMINO: A palomino horse is a gold color with a white mane, tail, and forelock.

9. ALBINO: An albino is white with pink skin and blue or brown eyes.

10. PINTO: The term pinto refers to a horse with white spots.

11. APPALOOSA: Appaloosa refers to color as well as to a breed of horse. The Appaloosa color comes in various patterns from large, colored spots the size of a fist to small flecks.

## MARKINGS

Horses are marked in a variety of ways, but the main ones are listed here.

1. BLAZE: A wide white stripe beginning at the horse's forehead, continuing down the face to the nose.

A blaze.

A stripe.

A star.

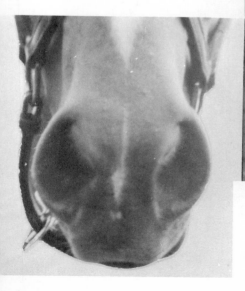

A snip.

2. STRIPE: A thin white blaze about the width of a pencil.

3. STAR: A white mark between the horse's eyes.

4. SNIP: A white mark between the horse's nostrils.

5. WATCH OR GLASS EYE: A blue eye. The lack of pigment does not affect the horse's vision.

6. STOCKING: White, starting at the horse's hoof (which will be white, too), and going up the leg. It ends just below the knee in front and the hock behind.

7. SOCK: A short stocking. The white usually goes a little above the fetlock joint.

8. BALD FACE: A blaze which comes down the horse's face and encircles his muzzle.

9. WHITE CORONET: A white marking around the coronary band (where the hoof joins the leg).

10. POINTS: Includes the mane, tail, forelock, and legs.

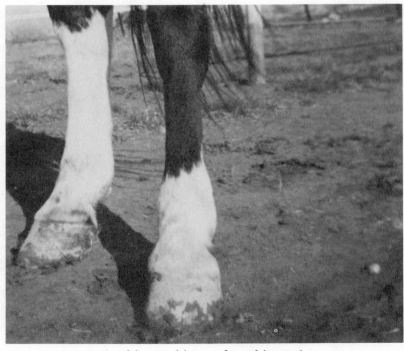

A white stocking and a white sock.

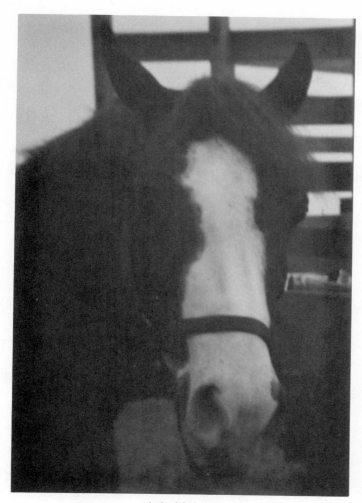

A bald face.

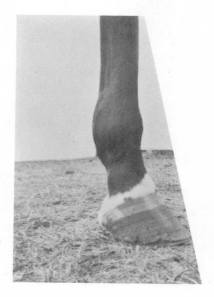

A white coronet.

# *Appendix B*

## CLOTHES FOR THE RIDER

For each type of riding there is a prescribed outfit which the rider must wear to be considered "correct."

The saddle seat attire is clothes worn by riders of all English horses for pleasure or show with the exception of the riders of the hunters and jumpers. These outfits are worn particularly by riders of American Saddlebreds, Morgans, Arabians, and Tennessee Walking Horses. At horse shows these horses are shown in the following classes:

1. English Equitation—saddle seat
2. Three Gaited Class (also known as a "Walk-Trot" Class)
3. Five Gaited Class
4. Tennessee Walking Horse Show and Pleasure Classes
5. English Arabian Classes
6. English Morgan Classes
7. English Pleasure Horse Class (Exception—those who show hunters and jumpers in these classes)
8. English Road Hack Class (Exception—same as No. 7)
   In the afternoon, or in informal shows, the rider wears as follows:
1. Kentucky jodhpurs—bell bottoms, no flare at sides
2. Matching or contrasting saddle seat coat—long coat with one vent and two pleats (must match for equitation classes)
3. White shirt
4. Bow tie or four-in-hand tie
5. Jodhpur boots—low boots
6. Derby—hard or soft

7. Gloves—optional, but they look nice
8. Flower in buttonhole—optional, but it looks nice
   In the evening, or in a formal show, the rider wears:
1. Tuxedo riding suit—black Kentucky jodhpurs with matching or contrasting coat, satin lapels, and satin stripe down pant legs

A saddle seat equitation rider correctly attired.

Jodhpur boots with elastic gore on left, and hunt boot on right.

(must match for equitation classes)
2. Black tie, boots, and gloves; high silk top hat
3. Flower in buttonhole
The color combinations for saddle seat attire are as follows:
1. Brown boots and hat with tan or brown suit
2. Black boots and hat with blue or black suit
3. Dark jodhpurs with a white, plaid, or brocade coat
4. Colorful vests look nice under a coat
5. Gloves can either match the suit or be white. They should be a thin leather. White gloves may show faults in the case of an equitation rider
6. The best principle to follow when selecting riding clothes is to choose quiet colors. A rider does not want to wear an outfit that will detract from his horse except in the case of Equitation Classes. Here the rider *does* want to be noticed. A bright flower, vest, or accessory is correct in this case.

The complete outfit for the rider of hunters, jumpers, and dressage horses.

Those who ride hunters and jumpers ride what is called the forward seat. The clothes for these riders are:

1. English breeches—pants with a flare side ending halfway down the calf of the leg
   a. First hunt season—tan or brown breeches
   b. White breeches with "Pink" coat (a red hunt coat tailored by an Englishman named "Pink")
   c. After the first season—yellow breeches with black coat
2. Black high boots—come to just below the knee
3. Coat:
   a. Black Melton (wool)—plain for the first season
   b. Ladies who are not members of the Hunt staff wear black coats with colored collars after their first season
   c. "Pink" coat—worn by men after their first season of hunting if they belong to a Hunt Club. It has special gold buttons with the initials of the Hunt Club on them

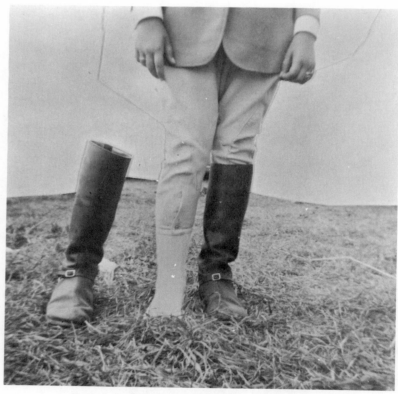

Breeches are worn with high hunt boots.

4. Hat:
     a. Hard hunt cap made of velvet is worn by the Master of the Hounds, the Hunt Servants, and children under eighteen. Those who are still novices wear the bow turned up
     b. High silk hat—formal type for members of the field; has hard reinforcement
5. Stock tie—tied in a special knot and pinned with a plain gold safety pin. This can serve as a sling or bandage in case of an accident

Those who pleasure ride can wear what they want when riding alone. However, here again a certain outfit bears the stamp of approval for riding in company.

A rider dressed for a pleasure pony class at a horse show.

These English jodhpurs are worn with low jodhpur boots for pleasure riding.

1. Breeches, Kentucky or English jodhpurs—English jodhpurs have flare sides and come down to the boot tops, ending in a cuff
2. Jodhpur boots with jodhpurs; hunt boots with breeches
3. Plaid, tweed, or solid color coat, usually wool
4. Derby—usually soft or hunt cap
5. Tie and white shirt or ratcatcher shirt
6. String gloves

# *Appendix  C*

TEST YOURSELF: What are the riders in the following illustrations doing incorrectly? The answers are on page 243.

1.

2.

3.

4.

5.

6.

ANSWERS

1. 1. The rider has her legs incorrectly turned so that the calves are constantly applying pressure. This could create problems with a high strung horse.
   2. The toes are out because of the way the rider has turned her calves.
   3. The ankles are stiff and inflexible.
   Bareback riders or those who attempt to teach themselves to ride often develop these leg problems.
2. 1. The rider's legs are too far forward.
   2. The rider is leaning back.
   3. The rider has rounded shoulders.
   4. The rider is leaning on the reins. If the reins were cut, the rider would fall back.
3. 1. The rider's reins are too long for good control.
   2. The rider's hands are too flat.
   3. The rider's legs are too far forward.
4. 1. The rider's legs are too far forward.
   2. The rider's shoulders are stiff and pulled up.
   3. The rider's heels are up.
   4. The rider's hands are flat.

5.  1. The rider is sitting too far back in the saddle.
    2. The rider's hands are too far back.
6.  1. The rider has rounded her shoulders.
    2. The rider is using the back of her calves. This results in knees and inner thighs away from the saddle and toes out— a weak leg position.

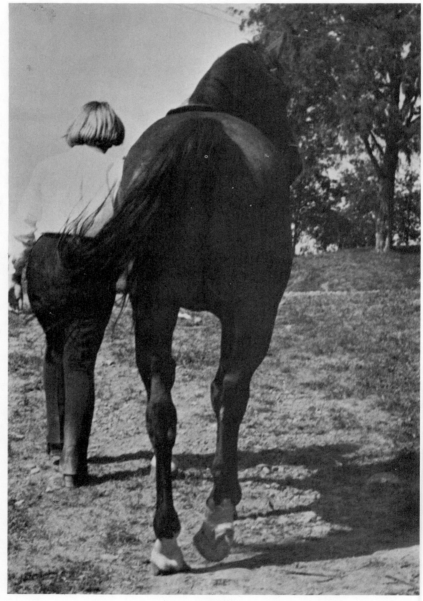

THE END

# Index